The Web
of Women's
Leadership

The Web of Women's Leadership

Recasting Congregational Ministry

Susan Willhauck & Jacqulyn Thorpe

Abingdon Press/Nashville

THE WEB OF WOMEN'S LEADERSHIP:
RECASTING CONGREGATIONAL MINISTRY

Copyright © 2001 by Abingdon Press

All rights reserved.
No part of this work may be reproduced or transmitted in any form or by any
means, electronic or mechanical, including photocopying and recording, or by
any information storage or retrieval system, except as may be expressly permitted by the 1976 Copyright Act or in writing from the publisher. Requests
for permission should be addressed to Abingdon Press, P.O. Box 801, 201
Eighth Avenue South, Nashville, TN 37202-0801.

This book is printed on acid-free paper.

Library of Congress Cataloging-in-Publication Data

Willhauck, Susan, 1955–
    The web of women's leadership: recasting congregational ministry /
Susan Willhauck & Jacqulyn Thorpe.
        p.   cm.
    Includes bibliographical references.
    ISBN 0-687-07296-4 (alk. paper)
    1. Christian leadership.   2. Women clergy.   I. Thorpe, Jacqulyn, 1942–
II. Title.

BV652.1 .W49 2001
262'.14'082—dc21   00-046909

Scripture quotations, unless otherwise indicated, are from the *New Revised
Standard Version of the Bible*, copyright 1989, Division of Christian Education of
the National Council of the Churches of Christ in the United States of
America. Used by permission. All rights reserved.

Scripture quotations noted *Message* are from *THE MESSAGE*. Copyright © Eugene
H. Peterson, 1993, 1994, 1995. Used by permission of NavPress Publishing Group.

Scripture quotations noted NASB are taken from the NEW AMERICAN
STANDARD BIBLE®, © Copyright The Lockman Foundation 1960, 1962,
1963, 1968, 1971, 1972, 1973, 1975, 1977, 1995. Used by permission.

Scripture quotations marked (NIV) are taken from the HOLY BIBLE, NEW INTER-
NATIONAL VERSION®. NIV®. Copyright © 1973, 1978, 1984 by International Bible
Society. Used by permission of Zondervan Publishing House. All rights reserved.

Scripture quotations noted KJV are taken from the King James or Authorized
Version of the Bible.

David M. Noer's "A Recipe for Glue" is from *The Leader of the Future*,
Hesselbein, Goldsmith, and Beckhard, eds. Copyright © 1996 by Peter F.
Drucker Foundation for Nonprofit Management. Reprinted by permission of
Jossey-Bass Inc., a subsidiary of John Wiley & Sons, Inc.

The excerpt of Julia Esquivel's "They Have Threatened Us with Resurrection"
is from *Threatened with Resurrection*. Copyright © 1994 by Brethren Press. Used
by permission of Brethren Press.

The lyrics for "Sing Oh Barren One" are BY BERNICE JOHNSON REAGON,
© Songtalk Publishing Co. (BMI). Used by permission.

01 02 03 04 05 06 07 08 09 10—10 9 8 7 6 5 4 3 2 1

MANUFACTURED IN THE UNITED STATES OF AMERICA

For our children
Dr. Crystal Thorpe, Constance Thorpe, Kimberly
Thorpe, and Jeff Thorpe
Hannah Willhauck and Stephen Willhauck

And for women and men in ministry everywhere

Contents

Preface

The decision to write this book was made over lunch in the refectory of Wesley Theological Seminary between two women who were both colleagues and friends who had not seen each other in a while and were catching up and sharing with each other some personal pain over the church. This was not ordinary whining, however, but deep-seated disappointment and despair over injustices toward women and other "marginalized" people in the church. One of us told about a book that had caused a breakthrough for her. The book focused on the metaphor of the web as a way of living and leading in organizations. We were excited, and we both agreed this story must be told to the church.

Perhaps you, too, have wished that the church could move away from the "command and control" structure and leadership that has, in our view, de-capacitated it. When we speak of the church, we mean both the church in general and local communities of faith. Our expression, we hope, is pluralistic, but it is also particular. Our "particularism" is in The United Methodist Church. We are told the "epidemic" is widespread across denominational lines, and the "virus" has many strains that are resistant to treatment. In church and denominational rhetoric, we sound as though we are moving away from oppressive structures, affirming the ministry of all baptized believers; but in reality, command and control still reigns.

In the church today, we have some people who "make it" in the church power structure and some who do not. Ego is a fact of human nature, and egos are allowed to inflate in the church, which places few restraints on positional power. Those who are successful often believe they deserve that success and good reputation simply because of their position. The fact that some individuals have "climbed the ladder" proves their worth, doesn't it? The truth is that in order to climb the ladder, many think they have to throw somebody else off to make room. The attitude that my success can only be precipitated by your failure is as prevalent in the church as it is in many institutions in our competitive society. Many people have been thrown off the ladder for various reasons, including those who tried to play by the rules. As female Christian educators in the church, we have been thrown off the ladder many times—so many times that we have sought alternative ways to be the church and lead in the church. The truth is, no matter what your "position" in the church, you are only as good as your ideas and your ability to carry them out.

We admit we are iconoclastic, seeking to dissolve some of the sacred cows of the church, but this book about women's leadership in the church is not a male-bashing or a church-bashing exercise. We recognize that men can and do exercise a weblike leadership, and we love the church and will remain loyal to it, even as we foster reform. We do not wish to be negative; indeed we have a lot of hope for the church, or we would not have bothered to write this book. One of us once received some unsolicited advice: "Never write a book in anger." Yet anger has fueled some of the noblest movements in history. We harbor no illusions that this book will start a movement, but we have made use of our anger, we hope, for good. We acknowledge that there is more than one right answer in regard to the questions surrounding the future of the church and leadership within it. This book is but one answer that comes from focusing and framing the big picture through the lenses of two women educators, and we entered into this partnership to share a new vision for Christian leadership in the church.

As we approached the daunting task of writing this book, our initial enthusiasm quickly turned to abject fear. Fear, at first, of all the overwhelming work involved in writing a book because both of us were already heavily committed to church and family responsibilities and seminary teaching, then the fear of how our message would be received. Ever confident in each other's abilities and bolstered by prayer, however, we plunged ahead—partly out of naive boldness, partly out of genuine courage, and partly out of the instinctive feeling that we were on to something that might resonate and serve to start a dialogue with and among church leaders.

We supported each other through the project—we hope modeling the spirit of a "web way of being" and exercising web leadership and pedagogy. When one of us faltered or became bogged down or dried up, the other one supported her and vice versa. We came to appreciate each other's inner beauty and strengths in new ways—Susan's poignant turn of phrase; Jackie's diligent "homing device" for picking up on relevant material and ideas, Susan's way of plumping out the message with both intellect and feeling, and Jackie's encyclopedic knowledge and theological understanding of ministry.

To be frank, one source of trepidation when we agreed to work together and after we signed the contract for the book was whether we would be able to live up to what we were proposing. Could two people of different backgrounds and experience, who had very different writing styles, write a book together? No less important was the question, Could an African American woman who was oppressed by whites and a white woman who was a Southerner by birth and a coconspirator in white oppression of blacks in the church, find common ground? Could we bridge our differences, could we bridge our different assumptions and perspectives on how to tackle this topic? At times, if we're honest, we admit we were skeptical. Our skepticism was not of each other (for we share a long friendship and common bond as Christians and church educators), but our fear and trembling was more unspoken. Was the bond of our sisterhood strong enough, and yet flexible enough, to hold when one of us challenged or questioned the other?

When one of us seemed clueless about the other's experience or perspective or even convictions about what this book should be, would the other be able to open up and see the value in that perceived "clueless-ness" as an opportunity for developing understanding, for fine-tuning the message, and for thinking outside the box? We wanted to model the web way of being in our writing. We wanted to blend our knowledge, skills, and experiences to both examine the church and offer help to its leaders. We wanted to weave our writing together to make it strong while retaining our distinctive voices. We firmly believe that this happened.

We believe there has got to be a better way, or ways, to be the church. At least one of us is in favor of disman-tling whole structures in a radical way to cull out the inequalities—to start an intentional forest fire, if you will. The beauty of nature is that tenacity of life—even-tually in burned-out areas new life somehow emerges. The fireweed, the first plant that feeds from the burned ashes, blossoms. If that sounds radical, good. If it does not, then you should write a book.

We believe that there is a better way, and that better

way, to us, is found in leadership that has its roots in an image for ministry conducive to a feminine way of being, which we are calling "the web." If you are interested (as we think you might be and hope you are) in a new way of being church, we would like to be in dialogue with you. We would like to offer ourselves to come to you and talk to your church or class about putting this into practice. We are interested in your response and your experiences with leadership in ministry and your faith community, because that is really "where it is at." A book can only suggest a method, spark an interest, or stimulate a discussion. The "trenches" is where we will succeed or fail. This is where the rubber meets the road. We envision workshops in churches, brainstorming sessions between clergy and laypeople, and without being too presumptuous, dialogue with the hierarchy—whom we do not personally consider to be the enemy, indeed some members of the upper echelon are working for change. In any case call, write, or E-mail one or both of us, or check out our website at www.webofwomensleadership.com. E-mail us with your examples of web leadership. We would love to talk with you because we know this is where it starts— not with us as the finders of the words, but with you and us as the doers of the Word.

Acknowledgments

We wish to thank the faculties and staff at Wesley Theological Seminary and Howard University School of Divinity. Their rich legacy of teaching, research, and church and community development has influenced, informed, and inspired us. We especially want to thank Dr. Bruce Birch, Dean of Wesley Theological Seminary, for his support and commitment to lay ministry, and our students at Wesley and Howard, from whom we have learned much. Thanks to the Reverend George Donigian from Upper Room Books for his help, encouragement, and friendship. We want to express appreciation to the staff at the General Board of Higher Education and Ministry of The United Methodist Church. Our thanks go to the church as well—the church who has nurtured, guided, bolstered, and sustained us in times of trial, and the church who has offered forgiveness and love to us, especially St. Matthew's UMC in Annandale, Virginia.

We express our deep gratitude to all the women who have been pioneers in ministry; we stand before these sisters in awe, and we want you to know: You will not be forgotten! Our sister friends at the American Association of University Women, in particular, have helped us over the years to focus on education and the well-being of women and girls in education. Thanks to all the women who served as role models for us and who serve as role models for girls and women everywhere in the church. A special thanks to Dr. Patricia Meyers for her blessed friendship.

Last, we thank our husbands: Marvin Thorpe, who shared the parenting of four children with Jackie, and Steve Willhauck, who, along with Hannah and Stephen, loved Susan through all this. We thank our readers and hope you will keep us in your prayers. We thank God for smiling on us and for bringing us peace.

CHAPTER ONE

The Web: What It Is and How It Feels

I am about to do a new thing; now it springs forth, do you not perceive it?

ISAIAH 43:19*a*

All things are connected. Whatever befalls the earth befalls the children of the earth. We did not weave the web of life; we are merely strands in it. Whatever we do to the web, we do to ourselves.

ATTRIBUTED TO CHIEF SEATTLE

You just have to find a way to stop doing what's stupid.

CHARLENE ELLIS,
QUOTED IN *THE WEB OF INCLUSION*

A Webster's dictionary definition says that a web is an intricate structure suggestive of something woven, a network, or a snare or entanglement. A web can be a beautiful interwoven tapestry of glistening fibers, but it can also be a tangled mess in which something gets irreversibly stuck. A web can get very complex and tangled and entangled; more and more, for today and tomorrow, the structure of life and work suggests a web to us.

In writing this book, we want to lift up the web as a metaphor of leadership for the church. The web image works, for example, as a model for how we should seek to make disciples. We know that life is no longer a simple pecking order, or a "top-down" way of being, but it is an intricate network of people, opportunities, and resources. Things simply do not and cannot work effectively from a top-down perspective any more. The web is the reality in which we live today. Used correctly, in its positive sense, web leadership offers a better way, as we hope to convince our readers.

One kind of web, to use an example from nature, is woven by the spider. Who has not witnessed one of these amazing, symmetrical creations strung between two far-flung trees, shimmering in the sunlight, sustaining droplets of dew? Who has not marveled at the hairlike thinness, as well as the tremendous strength, of the strands of the web? We want to dispel the myth of the spider as an evil and conniving creature. Spiders are, in fact, graceful, diligent, determined, industrious, creative, artistic, consistent, and persistent creatures. Their webs can teach us about and be symbols of new, far-reaching, and inclusive ministries.

We hear much about another kind of web, the World Wide Web, and though this web is an enigma to some, to more and more people who take advantage of the technology, "the Web" symbolizes the interconnectedness of the world. Microsoft Corporation's Bill Gates predicts that a constellation of refrigerator-size satellites will soon link every point on the globe in an explosion of interconnections.[1] The Web calls to mind our newfound ability to communicate with anyone, anytime, anyplace. It means the expansion of our knowledge, and we are no longer comfortable with the limitations, which in some cases were imposed on us by others, that kept us from knowing all we needed to know. It means we are now and forever *linked*, and we cannot go back to the old ways that kept us isolated. We are captivated by the Web, with its open communication and free-flowing information. The Web is appropriate for our time because its design and structure mirrors that of our technology of the integrated network.

A book by journalist Sally Helgesen entitled *The Web of Inclusion: A New Architecture for Building Great Organizations* uses the metaphor of the web to describe a system of management intended to replace the hierarchical system that she believes is limited, and limiting, when it comes to the effectiveness of an organization today. Helgesen describes a web as being a structure that is "roughly circular in shape" with concentric circles "bound together by . . . axial and radial lines that crisscrossed the structure in a kind of filigree." The web is both a metaphor and a process. It is a way of thinking and acting. The interweaving creates a structure that is "inextricably integrated and connected."[2]

Metaphor Versus Style

According to Sallie McFague, metaphors emerge out of experience to express the ineffable. Mary Elizabeth Mullino Moore reminds us that metaphors are usually simple, common, physical things used to point us toward a more complex concept. Metaphors are pathways for communicating truths that escape our attempts to verbalize, and they break open our "structures of expectation" and make us receptive to new and fresh insights.[3] Like Jesus' parables, "they make the familiar strange and shock us into new awareness."[4] "Root" metaphors ground us, give us our foundation, and keep us from being blown away by the latest fad that breezes by.

The web metaphor for leadership does not propose to be just one more approach or fad for the church. Rather, it seeks to embody the call for and the need for mainline churches to witness to the gospel by embracing those at the margins. Metaphors are not so much constructed by us as they are something we latch on to for guidance. We latch on to the metaphor of the web to describe our communal life. Communal life is threatened whenever we fail to see the interconnectedness, the bond that knits human relationships together.

> [We] spin visions of the ties between persons, which can best be suggested by the metaphor of the web and nets. Webs and nets imply opposing capacities for snaring or entrapment and for rescuing and safety. They also suggest a complexity of relationships and the delicate interrelatedness of all so that tension and movement in one part of the system will grow to be felt in all parts of the whole. In the complexity of a web, no one position dominates over the rest. . . .
>
> In contrast, the self promised in autonomy sees individuals relating through bonds of agreements, such as contracts, laws, and the like. Their metaphors for suggesting the world are more often images of pyramids and mountains. On the metaphorical mountain the few at the top dominate the many at the bottom. . . . Those on the mountain find it easier to maintain the view that some must lead and others must follow, that some will win while the rest will lose. In the hierarchical world that the players with these limited epistemologies construct, the game is rigged.[5]

One of the challenging but intriguing things about a metaphor is that it can usually be turned inside out; it can be viewed from a positive or negative stance. A spider web is strong. This is indeed a positive image. There is an old African proverb that says, "When spider webs unite, they can tie up a lion." Yet today we sometimes speak of the web of oppression, of being irretrievably caught in a trap of domination. At a symposium for Korean American ministry, Young Pai expressed this "two-eyed" view: "A web can be the place where one is

18

caught and is the victim, or it can be the place where one lives."[6]

The web metaphor, in its positive sense, helps us understand new leadership in the church. The web is a metaphor for leadership in general more than it is for any particular style of leadership. Certainly the web metaphor engenders particular styles, but we would not presume to say that all women leaders prefer to operate with a web style of leadership just as we would not say that men leaders do not. We want to dispel the "one size fits all" view of leading the church. There are many styles and expressions of leadership that are well grounded in theological and moral reflection. We simply offer the web as a way of looking at a new kind of leadership that utilizes what Sally Helgesen calls "the female advantage."[7] The metaphor of the web represents the possibility of change in the church that may be called for by the presence of women in leadership.

Women in Ministry

The presence of women in ministry and the reports of high enrollment of women in seminaries suggests a need for a change in church leadership structures that is more conducive to allowing women to lead in creative and new ways. *The Washington Post* reports that, nationally, 16,408 women described themselves as clergy in 1983. By 1996, according to federal labor statistics, 43,542 women did—making up 12.3 percent of all U.S. clergy.[8] Carol Becker's research for her book *Leading Women* confirmed that styles of leadership have multiplied since women have entered church leadership in significant numbers.[9] In some circles within the Christian community this same vocation seeks a new understanding of leadership that is based on the contributions of women. While the ordained ministry continues to be a male-dominated profession with only 12.3 percent being women, that percentage is still a significant indicator of change in the profession. There are enough female clergy to cause things to be done differently. Although there has been growth in the number of women pursuing and entering ministry, there is a concern that many of them will become discouraged and leave.

In the book *Women's Issues in Religious Education*, a chapter by Harriet Miller entitled "Human Development: Making Webs or Pyramids" summons new symbols of unity and inspires a quest for new symbols for developing Christian disciples. Miller alludes to the evolution of developmental theory, which in previous stages involved some unbalanced and hierarchical views of human development that were gender biased.[10] In addition, Carol Gilligan's well-known work on women's development fuels a passionate search for a new way of leading that does not threaten people and does not confine us to rule-bound and competitive situations. Gilligan found that women often make decisions based on relationship and caring.[11] Without stereotyping or attempting to articulate a unique feminine style, Carol Becker concludes that women leaders demonstrate clearly identifiable gifts and skills.[12] Using Mary Field Belenky's work on *Women's Ways of Knowing*, Becker identified some characteristics of women, such as a willingness to share information, the ability to negotiate, a concern for human relationships, the ability to juggle many tasks at once, and a preference for participatory management—all of these qualities are congruent with a more weblike style of leadership.

Sally Helgesen found, in her research, that women prefer leadership structures that clearly differ from the traditional form. She interviewed women in many diverse organizations and read their day-to-day logbooks and calendars. The structures devised by these women were very different from those she had encountered in other institutions, including schools, universities, political and charitable organizations, and the church. She found that these women exercised their freedom to devise ways of leading that made sense to them. They had built "integrated, organic," and transparent organizations in which the emphasis was on nurturing good relationships. Everyone could see what was happening. The pyramidal structure that was considered the norm played little part in this style of leadership, so Helgesen began to search for a new metaphor for a method of leadership that could transform organizations. Hence she focused on the web to portray several women's preferred way of leading.[13] The church needs the metaphor of the web to guide our ministry tasks as we enter the twenty-first century.

The Hierarchical Model

Two prototypes for the hierarchical model in the Western world are the military and the church.[14] As Christianity became the established faith of third-century Rome, an elaborate system composed of priests, bishops, and archbishops emerged—the ascending ranks being modeled perhaps on the ranks of angels. The very word *hierarchy* means "the rule of priests." It would seem that the word hierarchy is inherent in the church itself. Is the church's hierarchical system, then, inevitable? Some do accept it as a necessary evil.

The irony is that Jesus had the opposite of hierarchy in mind in calling disciples. Alexandre Faivre writes of Jesus' anticlericalism, or Jesus' rejection of human power that claimed to be absolute.[15] Jesus admonished the disciples for arguing among themselves about who was the greatest: "He sat down, called the twelve, and said to them, 'Whoever wants to be first must be last of all and servant of all' " (Mark 9:35).

Can the church not model the reign of God that Jesus planted in our imaginations? Jesus chose Peter to be the foundation for his church: "On this rock I will build my church" (Matt. 16:18). He chose Peter not as the greatest but as one on whose faith the church would be built. Peter was to be at the center of the web, and whatever he bound on earth would be bound in heaven. One advantage of the web over the hierarchical system is that the leader in the center can connect all around instead of just downward.

Critiquing the hierarchical system that developed in the church resembles the story *The Emperor's New Clothes*. A trickster convinced a king that he could make a suit of clothes that were so special that only wise people could see them. At first, when one honest boy pointed out that the king was indeed naked, all the bystanders were outraged. Soon, however, one by one, they had to admit the boy was telling the truth. When a truthful observer points out the obvious—something amiss that people have been denying—shock waves are sent through the community. We are still capable of being shocked at the revelation of the nakedness of the church.

The hierarchical structure of the church, we might say, is like a *Jurassic Park*, which houses a dinosaur that is out of place in today's world. It is big and cumbersome, and although it ought to be extinct, there are some who seek to preserve it at all costs. A hierarchical structure fosters a climate of uncertainty, suspicion, and rumor. The web structure, on the other hand, fosters communication and connectedness. Some members in a community or organization that functions as a hierarchical structure will always feel like outsiders who are "out of the loop."

Recent books, including Vashti McKenzie's *Not Without a Struggle*, Delores Williams's *Sisters in the Wilderness*, and Cheryl Sanders's *Saints in Exile*, document this marginalization, particularly in the experience of women. The tendency of hierarchical structures to ostracize those who do not "fit in" leads to the erosion, or the wearing down, of women in ministry, according to Delores Carpenter, professor of religious education at Howard University School of Divinity (whose forthcoming book will describe her research into this problem).

The Rolf Memming Longitudinal Clergy Study confirmed that women leave the local church ministry at a rate that is 10 percent higher than that of men. The Clergywomen Retention Study of the Anna Howard Shaw Center at Boston University School of Theology found data to indicate that reasons for leaving the ministry include lack of support from the hierarchical system.[16] Women have hit the "stained-glass ceiling" when it comes to succeeding in the male-dominated ministry, according to a University of Florida study based on a 1995 survey of 190 ordained United Methodist clergywomen across the United States.[17]

Apparently men are leaving too. Leonard Sweet writes about the number of veteran male clergy who are opting for retirement at the earliest possible age. Clergy are leaving faster than they are being replaced. He notes that something is not working and is not in touch with the times.[18] Increasingly, men, too, are disillusioned with the traditional chain of command leadership. Minorities have long felt this disillusionment, but now, people who have previously been part of the minorities are becoming the majority.

Some women leaders would prefer to put themselves at the center of their organizations, rather than at the top, but they feel they have to emulate the status quo in order to succeed. They look to the oppressors and repressors for accreditation. The women who have attempted to buy into the hierarchy in the church, "to be one of the big boys," compete with other women and often are not able to work in a collegial fashion. Regrettably, anecdotal evidence suggests that the woman-against-woman syndrome in the church has been pervasive and has not helped the effectiveness of women's leadership in ministry. Although women initially may have felt a need to compromise as they made inroads into the male establishment, surely now we can claim our own preferred ways of leading. Again, this is not to say that all women prefer weblike leadership, but when leaders "work out of the center" of their organizations or classrooms (as we shall see in "The Web and Pedagogy") and include others in the decision making in an interactive charisma or leadership, the leader derives power and authority from being accessible, since access allows one to shape information as it evolves.

In the hierarchical system, there is the sense that the power base of the church rests with a few. Web leadership is undermined by hierarchy because of the competition it creates. One "web leader" we know (we will call her Jan) became discouraged in a ministry setting because her supervisor was jealous of her connections, nationally and locally. Jan knew many people and knew how to get things done. Instead of working with her, the supervisor (also a woman) chose to exclude Jan and felt threatened by her. If she was allowed to use her connective leadership, Jan might soon "take over" and somehow climb above the supervisor. Jan, however, survived and successfully exercises her preferred connectional leadership in another setting where its benefits are recognized.

Our ministry and mission is limping along instead of charging ahead with the vigor of enthusiastic people in ministry for Christ. There is little sense of ownership for those who are not among the few in power in the chain of command. You wait to be led instead of leading. The church is one of the last few holdouts among institutions, and it is one of the few organizations still trying to make a dying structure come back to life. Helgesen cites some examples that indicate that the church lags behind the health care industry, the automobile industry, and even the military in some cases, in making necessary changes to move away from the hierarchical system.

Clergy and Laity in the Church

Efforts through the centuries to question the hierarchy and reform the church involved a resurgence of the laity and grassroots movements. The term *lay*, or *laos*, means people and originally referred to all the people of God, including clergy and those who were not clergy. There is no trace of the notion of lay as distinct from ordained in the New Testament, no biblical ordering of the church into clergy and laity.[19] *Kleros*, the word from which *clergy* derives, was also applied to the whole people of God.

In the earliest Christian communities there was no independent priestly function exercised by a special class. It was not until the end of the first century that the term *laikos*, used to describe those who were not clergy, appeared in the writings of Clement of Rome. By the third century *kleros* referred to a limited group within the Christian community.[20] There was conflict in the churches around institutional order. Ranking became a way to establish that order. Order and harmony are still good; ranking, however, is no longer an effective way to achieve that order. Ranking, on the contrary, creates disorder and rebellion.

Current usage of the word *lay* denotes one who is not a professional or one who is untrained. That usage, however, is a distortion of the word's original meaning. In the early Christian community, *laos* frequently expressed an important theological concept referring to the Old Testament designation of Israel—not simply a crowd or mass of people, but a unity, a union, a chosen people. Even the development of an official priesthood did not nullify the fundamental task of that unity. Church historians describe the early church as a movement in which all baptized people were active in the church's mission demonstrated by Paul's description in 1 Corinthians 12 of differences in function that stem from the different gifts given by the Spirit.

By the second century, there was an increasing trend toward clericalism and a subordination of the nonordained. Apostolic succession was the term that developed for the link each priest had with the original apostles chosen by Jesus, a link that came to denote power, privilege, and authority rather than service. Clericalism, or the inappropriate giving of high rank or status to the ordained, is elitist, and as such, it is as dangerous today as ever. Clericalism affects spirituality. Once the clergy became identified with the realm of the sacred, the laity were considered profane—a misunderstanding that fostered, and still fosters, an unhealthy dualism. The laity are encouraged to expect that ministry will be directed *to* them and *for* them. This form of ministry inevitably becomes self-serving and directed inward toward the preservation of the institution, a "maintenance-mode" way of ministry that neglects the ministry to the world, causing a false dichotomy between the sacred and the secular spheres. Worship resembles a "filling station," and teaching becomes "banking education,"[21] with faith becoming fideism or mindless assent. A true understanding of liturgy, however, requires that we affirm worship as the "work of the people," not the clergy.

By the end of the fourth century bishops had gradually ceased to be tied to a particular church as shepherd or husband to that community and began to make careers for themselves by moving about and striving to become bishop of a province or capital. Bishops came to be viewed as "princes" of the church who associated with other leading public figures. Many bishops developed a taste for temporal power. The fourth century saw a proliferation of clergy. There were so many that a hierarchical organization parallel to that of civil administration developed. These organizations took most of their metaphors from the navy, the army, or educational structures. These comparative hierarchies attempted to rationalize and justify the value of an ascending scale within the church's orders and the reasons for striving to climb it. All Christian authority came to be regarded as having direct divine authority, and therefore, the higher one ascended, the more divine authority that person was thought to have.[22]

One of the agendas of the Reformation, along with Martin Luther's "priesthood of all believers," was a reclaiming of the proper and authorized role of the laity as a corrective to the corruption among the hierarchy. Following the Reformation, however, the church did not always make good on the promise and failed to implement the leadership of the laity adequately.

Most males in the United States born before 1950 were either drafted or volunteered for the military and had their first work experience in a hierarchical and bureaucratic setting. They learned organizational and management practices that they carried with them to their future careers, including the ministry. The male-dominated leadership in the church contributed to the excessive hierarchical nature. The late-1950s saw a post–World War II resurgence of the laity with the publication of Hendrik Kraemer's *A Theology of the Laity* (1958) and continued with the work of Richard Niebuhr, *The Purpose of the Church and Its Ministry* (1956), and Findley Edge, *The Greening of the Church* (1971).

Even the hierarchy can recognize the decline and stagnation of a church without an empowered laity. In fact "enabling," "equipping," and then "empowering" came to be buzzwords in ministry circles in the 1970s and 1980s. For many Christian educators, this vision of enabling laity for leadership was an attempt to get laity to accept more responsibility and ownership, but the sense that emerged was that clergy and staff had to give the laity what they lacked. The laity lacked power. The laity were "disabled."

Other efforts to revive the laity came from evangelical movements like Walk to Emmaus, the lay witness mission movement, and long-term Bible studies—some of which are sanctioned by the hierarchy. These ministries are acceptable to the hierarchy, as long as the laity "know their place." The motivation for reviving lay leadership was the reduction of some of the clergy's work load rather than a true desire to strengthen lay ministry. Mary Collins concluded, "The clerical class within the church came into being as an event of history. There was a time when it was not. . . . It is not clearly the case that the historical emergence and persistence of a clerical class has worked to the well being of the church."[23] We forget that clergy are first laypersons. Tertullian pointed out in the third century that it is the laity who give rise to the priests, not the other way around. Rather than two poles of clergy and laity, he recognized that the priests come forth from among a robust laity, and Tertullian was known to castigate bishops who forgot this fact.[24]

Despite the continued questioning of the church hierarchical system, which regulates the laity to a subordinate position, actual change is slow. Ten years ago Maria Harris, a Roman Catholic religious educator, wrote that the clergy-laity form of being the church is undergoing drastic revision. She wrote that the church is a people with a pastoral vocation. To assume that only the ordained are pastors is wrong. She wrote:

> The language of "clergy" and "laity" is less and less appropriate today, precisely because it does not attend to the symbolic reality it attempts to convey. The ordained and the nonordained are not related as haves and have-nots, as sacred and secular, as illuminati (enlightened

ones) and ignorant. Instead, our differing roles are com-
plementary to one another and often overlapping. As
never before, except perhaps in New Testament times,
the far more appropriate symbolism is of a people, where
some are "apostles, some prophets, some evangelists,
some pastors and teachers," but all are together for the
building up of the body of Christ.[25]

Today, we still do not embody the relationship
between clergy and laity that she described. Those who
are at the middle or bottom of the pyramid feel left out,
isolated, and alienated. They are not responding to the
leadership of the church. In the old metaphor of the
melting pot, in which we aim for uniformity and assert
that "the cream will rise to the top," the reality (familiar
to many cooks) is "that which is on the bottom gets stuck
to the pan and burned."

The church is in trouble. Not only are people leaving and
numbers declining, the church is losing its influence on
society and individuals.[26] Church leaders frantically seek
ways to improve the ministry of their congregations in
order to stop the drop in membership. Many try the latest
church growth strategies. Those leaders whose primary
goal is increasing numbers might advocate web leadership
solely for "marketing" purposes, reasoning that this type of
management has helped increase sales in business, so
therefore, in the church this style of leadership could be
used for the purpose of gaining members. That motivation,
however, is not the primary reason for adopting the web
leadership metaphor. Although changing our way of leading might help alleviate the decline in membership and dis-
engagement of people from the church, the merit of this
metaphor stands mostly in its integrity as a way to describe
our shared life together and the leadership within it.

As Christians seek to rethink the meaning of "church"
in light of cultural changes and differences, part of that

pondering must involve asking what kind of leadership is needed in today's church. There is, however, hope that comes in the renewal and reclaiming of the diaconate. The Order of Deacon could possibly bridge the gaps between clergy and laity and church and world. Deacons will serve as models for laypeople in action, embodying servant ministry and leading the laity to do Christ's work in the world. (More will be said later in this book about the diaconate and its effect on the hierarchical system.) Urgent work must be done, however, in order to implement and encourage the functioning of the new order, and that work includes the education of the church.

The Architecture of the Web

Margaret Wheatley observed in *Leadership and the New Science* that we are engaged in a search for "new sources of order for our world."[27] Helgeson suggests that the architecture of the web is one of those sources. Architecture is a science and an art that skillfully relates individual parts to a greater whole, creating a structure that is uniquely suited for a particular function. The old architecture of the pyramid is no longer functional. The most obvious architectural characteristic of the web is that it builds from the center out, and this building is a never-ending process. "The architecture of the web works as the spider does, by ceaselessly spinning new tendrils of connection, while also continually strengthening those that already exist."[28] In the web, the structure is continually being built up, stretched, altered, and transformed. At the outer edges the web is permeable and loose, which allows contact between those on the edge and those in the center. Leadership tools are not forced to develop into the ability to give commands, but they are developed to encourage access and dialogue. The flexibility and permeability builds strength, since the persons on the outer edge are as integral as those at the center, and those at the center move out to the edge as those at the edge move in to the center.

In the church, the ministry of those "on the edge," the leading edge, is truly effective and follows a ministry model that is most consistent with the teachings of Jesus. Branching out beyond the institution, doing new things, bringing the word into new areas, taking the church into the world, working on urgent needs, and transforming the role and image of the church are what truly matters. Richard Bondi wrote of a ministry at the edge versus a ministry at the center in his book *Leading God's People*. Cheryl Sanders wrote similarly of "a ministry at the margins."[29] Her work reflects a liberation model for ministry where the marginalized lead the way. What Bondi means by a ministry from the center is different from the concept of leadership from the center in the web image. For him ministry from the center remains hierarchical and is concerned with perpetuating and maintaining the institution in order to preserve an agreed upon point of view shared by those in power. In his view, ministry from the edge, on the other hand, is concerned with ministry in the world. In the image of the web, because the web is flexible, ever-changing, and loosely construed, the leader can be both at the center and at the edge. Because the ministry of those on the periphery truly does matter in the web model, they have more incentive for heartfelt participation than those somewhere in the rank and file of a pyramidal system where leadership is based on longevity.

Power and Its Sources

The matter of power is paramount in leadership. The *Dictionary of Pastoral Care and Counseling*, recognizing the importance of power in ministry, included an entry on power defining it as: "The ability to act or to be acted upon. A psychologically, socially, philosophically, and morally necessary part of our personal and social experiences, it is also open to great abuse."[30]

Some believe that the use of power is not an acceptable strategy for creating change in the Christian community, yet we know this happens all the time. Reinhold Niebuhr once said that all power is at some level corrupt. Perhaps this is true, but we all need power to get anything done. We have to have power to give us energy and light among other things. Leadership without power is like an automobile without an engine. The issue here is the *kind* of power we use. Those of us who are or who have been the victims of an abuse of power want to wish it away, but we admit that power is necessary to lead.

Studies from the Institute for Social Research have delineated coercive power, positional power, expert power, reward power, informational power, and connectional or relational power. Coercive power is based on fear or force alone and involves a use of power at its most corrupt level. Positional power is the power that one has simply by being in a certain position or office. Reward power is the leader's ability to bribe or reward to get things done. Of course, if the leader does not have access to adequate resources, if he or she cannot give raises or incentives, the power to reward is very limited. Informational power comes from possession or access to valuable information that is available only to a few. This suggests "keeping secrets," and as we indicated previously, power that depends on privileged information may soon be neutralized by the expanding of communications technology. Expert power is based on the leader's expertise or skill. This kind of power unfortunately may lead to competitiveness and vying for recognition as the best in one's field. It can also tempt some leaders, who think they need to put others down in

JESSIE C. EURY LIBRARY

I-Share Condition Report

This item was received at Jessie C. Eury Library in the following condition:

____✓ New/Good
____ Fragile
____ Loose/Torn Pages
____ Cover Torn/Worn/Bent
____ Binding Broken
____ Water Damage
____ Stained Pages
____ Marker/Pen/Pencil
____ Other:_____

Checked by: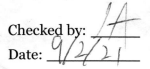
Date: 9/2/21

Jessie C. Eury Library
Lincoln Christian University
100 Campus View Dr.
Lincoln, IL 62656
217.732.3168 ext. 2234
library@lincolnchristian.edu
ILDS: LCC

Please do not remove this checklist.

Due: _____

Important notice for all patrons regarding items from I-Share libraries:

This item has been loaned to you from one of the 91+ libraries belonging to CARLI, the Consortium of Academic and Research Libraries in Illinois.

You are subject to the owning institution's loan and fine policies.

Failure to return or renew this material by the due date may result in processing fees, lost book charges, or overdue fines. Returning this book in a poor condition or failing to pay the lending institution's fines may result in a suspension of borrowing privileges.

To renew, visit the link below and click on "My Account."

libguides.lincolnchristian.edu

order to build themselves up, to judge and evaluate others harshly. Connectional or relational power is power with a more positive source and one that offers possibilities for the good of the community. This kind of power comes from connections that one has both inside and outside an organization. The connections do not need to be only with the influential; a wise leader understands that everybody can learn something from everybody else. Strong relationships can multiply an individual's power, but the point of acquiring power is not to benefit only the individual but to strengthen the community as a whole. It seems at times, however, that in the church as well as in the larger society, that the strong, charismatic, deserving leader has been replaced by "corporate raiders and other folks who live by the Darwinian law of survival."[31]

Harrison Owen, an Episcopal priest, theorizes that as the structures of our world cave in and certainty gives way to an "avalanche of change" our longing for strong leadership feels like a lost cause. The fault lies within our expectations. In the past, leaders served to make sense of chaos, to fix things, to make certainty out of doubt, and to create action plans. Now, however, there is no fixing chaos. Chaos is normal, and certainty is rare—if not impossible. Leadership that attempts to fix this can only fail.[32] We believe that has happened and is happening in the church. Some in the church may crave a strong, CEO-type leader who will fix things and create harmony and excellence, but this kind of leadership serves to create a membership that is dependent. More than likely, harmony cannot be imposed, and the leader wears himself or herself out trying.

In the hierarchy of the church, the priests were the ultimate owners of positional power. Early on, priests were thought to possess special, almost godlike magical powers. A semblance of this notion of special powers

33

continued throughout history and leaves its legacy even today. In the web, however, leadership from the center and the margins can help to reshape the concept and practice of power so that power is used for positive change. Power is the fuel that makes the system work, and it can be a source for needed change. However, *positional* power is no longer as effective as a power source as *relational* power. Respect and admiration for clergy has declined in our age, we believe, in no small measure because of the distrust of authority and positional power. Simply because a person holds a particular office or position is no longer seen as a reason to follow that person or do what they suggest. We are a society that questions authority. Harrison Owen wrote of his own experience:

> Although it is true that I have held positions with at least the appearance of formal power and authority attached, I can honestly say that I have never accomplished anything of significance through the use of such authority. There always seemed to be a better and, in many ways, simpler way, which I can call only the way of Spirit. . . . When it comes to leadership, the connection with Spirit is essential. Leadership in the absence of Spirit just does not make it. And Spirit simply refuses to play by somebody else's rules, as in "command and control."[33]

Barbara Brown Zikmund, Adair T. Lummis, and Patricia M. Y. Chang raise the issue of clergywomen and power in *Clergywomen: An Uphill Calling* and describe two leadership styles. One is transactional, which is the traditional "power over" method involving command and control leadership. A second style is "power with," or shared leadership style. Whereas many clergy say they would like to exercise a "power with" style, they sometimes give up when they find that building a consensus requires more time for making decisions, and they are discouraged when laypeople appear to lack interest in decision making.[34] Habits of church life are deeply embedded, and the habit of being passive "clients" is hard to break. Acknowledging that shared leadership is difficult, however, does not provide a good argument for rejecting it.

We are seeing signs, however, that web leadership is working and habits are changing. Zikmund, Lummis, and Chang found in their research that clergy (both women and men) perceive that women prefer shared leadership. According to the authors, the shared leadership approach can be seen as stereotypically "female," a perception that can undermine women's authority.[35] On the other hand, shared leadership, practiced by both women and men, is neither nonassertive nor wishy-washy. We would add that there is also the power from within that enables Paul to claim: "I can do all things through him who strengthens me" (Philippians 4:13). It is drawing from inner spiritual resources and from the resources of the *koinonia*, like drawing water from a well, that gives leaders collective strength. The publisher of the *Miami Herald* was quoted as saying, "If people don't feel they're participating in the decisions that affect them, they'll never really give you their best effort. . . . People are different now—they'll leave if they don't like how they're treated, and this is especially true of younger people."[36]

Connectional or relational power is becoming a far greater power than positional power. Helgesen says that the aggrandizement of purely positional power leads organizations to fall prey to a heroes-and-drones syndrome, which deprives those who have not achieved top rank of autonomy and motivation. This attitude is reflected in the demoralizing slogan of a few years ago, "Lead, follow, or get out of the way." Relational power is shared power. The web creates enduring and strong networks that balance the power in the organization. The leader creates an alternate center of power, usually outside the leader who is at the center of the web. This alternate power, however, is not a threat to the leader at the center but a powerful tentacle of the leader at the center's power. Like the engine within the automobile, this kind of relational and shared power takes you somewhere. If we continue to lead the church in the ways that we have during the twentieth century, we might not ever get there.

Helgesen describes the transformation of several organizations, like the *Miami Herald* newspaper, that occurred when they moved to a more weblike structure.

> It became vividly apparent that, by uniting people on issues that cut across usual boundaries of division and rank, the task force [using the web structure] . . . had helped transform the nature of the *Herald*. It had done this not least by creating rich reservoirs of nonpositional power among a wide diversity of people—people at every level in the organization. It was power that could be exercised in the cause of further change until positions opened up that defined power and made it tangible. It was a step: it brought maturity and understanding to people in the organization.[37]

Any perceived shift in power is threatening to those in power. Weblike leadership and ministry demanded by today's computer technology may be threatening to the hierarchy. "Unofficial" web sites and chat lines for those in ministry, not sanctioned by the various denominations, worry the bureaucracy of the church. Because knowledge is power, electronic information systems that create channels of communication, which transfer the power of expertise and knowledge, dilute the power of those in positions of authority. Communication is a tremendous source of power. While ostensibly embracing the technology, the hierarchy is fearful of it and sometimes drags its feet in making it available.

Here is an illustration, taken from events in the life of the church, of the fear that any perceived shift in power might cause. In November 1993, when women ministers gathered to celebrate, worship, dialogue, and network in Minneapolis at the Re-Imagining Conference, there was a great deal of negative publicity and fallout. At first the controversial issue seemed to be that the women were engaged in allegedly heretical worship practices. Word spread that they were worshiping "the goddess," and rewriting the Bible with a feminist slant. Some reports even indicated that witchcraft was being practiced. Actually, the real problem may have been the issue of power. Perhaps the real source of the controversy was that women were gathering and networking, activities that might result in more power for women in the church. Perhaps they were perceived as establishing a "block vote." Few of the critics liked the idea of a bunch of women getting together celebrating ministry. Were they planning a subversive takeover of the church? Suspicions ran high, and the anger and hurt that followed is only one example of the fragmentation in the church today, which is instilled by the "power at the top" and sealed off by fear.

Personal Success Versus Shared Vision

Both the hierarchical structure and the web structure are mutually reinforcing, meaning they both become more like themselves over time. The architecture of both structures determines how people will relate and how the structures function thus reinforcing itself. This is one reason that some efforts to get rid of a hierarchical system have failed. We are too ingrained in it. One woman educator related an experience that illustrates the difficulties of overcoming the system's entrenched dependence on hierarchical leadership. She once encouraged a male layperson that she worked with to pursue a call to ministry because she recognized the gifts for ministry in this person. This layperson had been active in the local church's educational and contemporary music ministries and had exemplified good leadership and a connectional style. She felt that in many ways she had "trained" this person to be an effective leader in the church. Several years later, however, after this person went to seminary and became a pastor, he changed drastically. Suddenly, he was her boss, telling her what to do, instituting policy for the church, and insisting on the letter of the law. He later "dissed" her and her work as he rose to the top. Several older women, pioneers in the corporate world during the 1970s, shared similar stories of training new male recruits only to have these same men rapidly surpass them in the system.

Many people in hierarchical organizations have become invested in doing and defending what has been done because it justifies what they have been doing. But many have recognized that the system is broken. Piecemeal efforts to replace the hierarchical system have not often work. The team ministry approach in church leadership may have been one such effort. While the philosophy of team ministry sounded good to many, it did not work the way it was intended. Lines of communication became blurred. Team members did their own thing as "loose cannons" in the church. While sports teams want to work together to win, there is also the disposition to produce "stars," or people who shine above the others. Like sports teams, large church staffs, instead of working together, often found themselves competing to see who could put on the best, most well-attended program. Who is the best at what they do? Who scores the most? Who gets the front page of the newsletter? Who gets the biggest budget? Things get out of hand—an example of the entanglement that can occur. The result is often an over-programmed church with a divisive and fragmented staff—busy, but not really reaching and transforming the lives of people. According to Eugene Peterson in *Subversive Spirituality:*

> Busyness is the enemy of spirituality. It is essentially laziness. It is doing the easy thing instead of the hard thing. It is filling our time with our own actions instead of paying attention to God's actions. It is taking charge. . . .
> I hate this professionalization of the church's ministry where the pastor hogs the show all the time. The laity should be committed to doing the real ministry of the church and the pastor should be committed to the spiritual direction of the laity.[38]

This inequity is illustrated further in the fact that regional denominational governing bodies (conferences) have little or no money for the education and training of laity. Most of their investment and funding goes into the training of clergy in order to fill pulpits. What does this say about our church? It also appears that some clergy do not want the laity to be educated and trained. They do not want laity to have the same access to the information and learning the clergy had because it closes the gap between expert and amateur. They do not want the layperson to "get ahold of the teacher's manual."

Robin Maas warns of the problems that the creation of stars in ministry provokes in *Crucified Love.* She writes that the emphasis on personal success and effectiveness in ministry, prevalent even in seminaries,[39] causes what we call the "lone ranger syndrome." Mother Teresa is credited with saying, "God did not call us to succeed, God called us to serve." Ministry is not about being a personal success; it is a process of serving and transforming. Henri

Nouwen writes about the "temptation to be spectacular" in *In the Name of Jesus*.

> I came to see that I had lived most of my life as a tightrope artist trying to walk on a high, thin cable from one tower to the other, always waiting for the applause when I had not fallen off and broken my leg. . . .
>
> When you look at today's Church, it is easy to see the prevalence of individualism among ministers and priests. Not too many of us have a vast repertoire of skills to be proud of, but most of us still feel that, if we have anything at all to show, it is something we have to do solo. You could say that many of us feel like failed tightrope walkers who discovered that we did not have the power to draw thousands of people. . . . But most of us still feel that, ideally, we should have been able to do it all and do it successfully. Stardom and individual heroism, which are obvious aspects of our competitive society, are not at all alien to the Church. There too the dominant image is that of the self-made man or woman who can do it all alone.[40]

Although team ministry was perhaps an attempt to get away from this "rugged individualist" approach, it proved to be a somewhat superficial answer. The difference between a team ministry approach and the web is that a team is task oriented, trying to achieve particular ends, to produce particular results or programs. The web structure focuses on the people and relationships rather than tasks. Process is emphasized, so everyone in the organization is seen as moving—not going after tasks, but sharing a desire for transformation and commitment. The health care industry provides an example. In the old hierarchical system where there was a compartmentalization of tasks, a single nurse would handle one task such as the giving of baths to all the patients on a ward; since this is an unglamorous task, it was usually given to the younger, more inexperienced nurses. In the new system, tasks were integrated and all duties involving a patient were assigned to one nurse, thus emphasizing the care of that person. This gave the primary nurse for a particular patient the time to get to know that person and gain valuable information and insight into proper care.

The web structure is organic, grass roots, "homegrown"; those in leadership help each other succeed. This organic process is known as *syntropy*, defined by biologists as the tendency of life to seek relationships, communication, and cooperation. People in relationship are not looking out for themselves, but they are concerned for the purpose of the organization and the actualization of a shared vision. The result of such ownership of a common vision and shared power is more loyalty to the organization, less turnover, more enduring and productive relationships inside and outside the organization, and more job satisfaction.

Improvisation and Transformation

Another characteristic of the web is the reliance on trial and error to get things done. The structure allows for the practice of what the Japanese call *kaizen*, or the art of making continual improvements and refining. Webs rely on improvisation, which is "thinking on your feet," inventing or composing extemporaneously, making use of what is conveniently at hand. This kind of resourcefulness is supposedly characteristic of American ingenuity, which is exemplified in the nature of America's indigenous art form: jazz.[41] The improvisation of jazz allows for individual expression *and* group allegiance. All contribute to the whole effect. According to Helgesen, "There's a saying among jazz musicians: 'don't make it up if it doesn't help.' In other words, express yourself only when it contributes to the larger effort."[42]

The resulting effect of the balance between individual expression and group endeavor is a transformed piece. Conflicting parts are now a whole. There is an interdependence in which all share in the failures and successes, and there is the sense that "God isn't finished with us yet," that there is grace and forgiveness for our imperfections. Improvisation glorifies diversity and differences coming together. Diversity, which is the subject of our third chapter, is the antithesis of balkanization, or the aligning of like-minded groups who are out for themselves. The beauty of the web structure is the constant flux, the continued opportunity for involvement and change.

The church could benefit from improvisation as opposed to bureaucratic, highly structured chains of command. Improvisation could allow the church more freedom to explore cutting edge ministries, and the opportunity for clergy-laity distinctions to go away. Diversity could be seen as a gift and blessing and not just tolerated or "something to be worked on," not something relegated to a "diversity department" but an attitude. It means that all leaders and all staff have responsibility for the whole rather than just "their area." Staff meetings are forums for shared decision making. Strict specialization and territorialism in ministry is replaced with broader approach in which people function in different ways and accept varying responsibilities. This freedom of self expression creates autonomy but not fragmentation. This vision will be further developed in this book.

One caution is in order here. We need to guard against the "frontier mentality" that has personified some of the high-tech companies that have planned the obsolescence of expensive equipment. Ethical issues are involved in the greedy and competitive attempt to produce the "product of the moment." This is manifest in the church in the faddishness that exists in ministry. Status-seeking—jumping to one "cause of the moment" or another, trying to be the first church on the block to be in some form of ministry in order to enhance one's status—has plagued religious institutions from the beginning. Sometimes our motives are pure, but we move in too quickly, thinking we can fix every problem. Henri Nouwen calls this pitfall the "temptation to be relevant,"[43] the attempt to be useful in order to fulfill the need of the moment. True transformation in the church will not come about with "fly-by-night" quick-fixes, but the art of improvisation with its trial and error can help us recognize and reach the kind of transformation that is called for in the church to live out the reign of God planted in our imaginations by Jesus Christ. Improvisation is not the end but the means. We invite you to imagine and explore the web in the church and to dialogue with us about what it means for our future.

Connect Questions

- Have you seen weblike leadership in operation? How might you describe its benefits and limitations?

- Now that women clergy have been around for a while in many denominations, what changes have you seen in the church that might be the result of their leadership?

- What are some of the effects of clericalism, and where have you witnessed this? How might traditional clergy and lay "ways of being" be transformed by web leadership?

- What are some challenges that women leaders in ministry will face in the near future?

CHAPTER TWO

The Web and Spiritual Unity

And who knoweth whether thou art come to the kingdom for
such a time as this?
ESTHER 4:14, *ORIGINAL AFRICAN HERITAGE BIBLE*
KING JAMES VERSION

Only, live your life in a manner worthy of the gospel of Christ,
so that, whether I come and see you or am absent and hear
about you, I will know that you are standing firm in one spir-
it, striving side by side with one mind for the faith of the
gospel.
PHILIPPIANS 1:27

Spiritual Unity and Current Disunity

For the church, spiritual unity means serving God
with a sense of oneness because we believe that we are
the Body of Christ and individually members of it. In
spite of this belief there is serious divisiveness. Not only
are there the centuries-old dissension between Catholic
and Reformed traditions, between the denominations,
and between conservatives and liberals; there is not only
historical and cultural divisiveness, there is tremendous
disunity *within* many denominations. Popular author
M. Scott Peck asserts that community and unity are cur-

45

rently rare commodities.[1] Several decades supporting values of individualism have contributed to this divisiveness, which is both theological and sociological with conflicting understandings of God's intentions and our role as Christians in the world and with differing ways of exercising our gifts for Christian leadership.

It is not extreme to say that most church infrastructures have been designed, built, reformed, and implemented with little input from women. This is not to belittle the contribution of women to the church, but simply to acknowledge a reality that—despite the great presence and leadership of women in the church, which is outlined in such books as Karen Jo Torjesen's *When Women Were Priests*[2] and Catherine Wessinger's *Religious Institutions and Women's Leadership*[3]—the church still operates from male-created order or hierarchy and theological perspectives that diminish or blatantly reject female leadership.

Mary Collins, O.S.B. testifies to the persistence of a classical clerical culture in her own Roman Catholic tradition. She claims the church was influenced by a culture grounded in imperial Roman public order: "It is a culture that refuses to allow the presence of women at its center and refuses to receive all the gifts of women. . . . [That culture] is distinguishable from the various cultures of western Europe in which Christianity took root and . . . flourished."[4] Despite the ordination of women in the Reformed and Evangelical traditions, women are still not easily received into the center in those traditions.

Vashti McKenzie, the first female bishop in the African Methodist Episcopal Church and author of *Not Without a Struggle*, discusses theological perspectives that support and reject female leadership. She says that the traditional male-articulated arguments that stem from Karl Barth's minimizing human experience and elevating only the Word of God as the starting point for theologi-

cal discourse do not speak to most women. Some liberation and feminist theologians contend that the experience Christian theology is formed out of is not a
universal experience but the experience of the dominant
culture. The experiences of women, African Americans,
Latinos, and other oppressed peoples are not considered.[5] In other words, theological method and spiritual
formation can no longer be pursued solely from Western
or North American perspectives.

Cain Hope Felder raises the same issue in his ground-
breaking book *Troubling Biblical Waters* when he talks
about Afrocentrism, which places Africans and those of
African descent as proactive participants in history and
theology rather than passive subjects. They become cen-
ters of value without being diminished or diminishing
any other group. In his opinion, Western Eurocentric theology has not done this.[6] James Cone in *God of the
Oppressed* said that God, the subject of theology, is eter-
nal. Those who articulate it are not. The language of theology is limited by history and time. It is not sensitive to
the ideas, purposes, or assumptions of a particular
group of people. Therefore, it is not universal.[7]

The rejection of the female experience or the African
American experience or the experience of other cultures
in theology has resulted in defective understandings of
effective leadership in ministry. Even though some
works on leadership from the 1980s and 1990s, such as
A Theology of Church Leadership by Lawrence O. Richards
and Clyde Hoeldtke and *Quest for Quality* by Ezra Earl
Jones, assert a need for more organic and relational leadership, that kind of leadership (while it can be pointed to
in isolation) has not yet taken root in the church.

Now, however, women's leadership in the church has
come to a turning point. There is an old saying in feminist circles: "The master's tools will never dismantle the
master's house." Trying to get ahead in a man's world

with equal access to education, jobs, and money was a goal of early feminists, and there is still a long way to go to accomplish that goal. Women felt (and some still do) that they had to compete with men on men's turf in order to get ahead. More and more women found that "the master's tools" were ineffective for them. The master's house (meaning the male-dominated church) needed to be torn down. You cannot do that by using the master's tools, by playing the game his way. Many women tried and failed to get ahead using the "master's tools." They discovered a way of leadership that seems right within their spirit, a caring, connectional weblike leadership that allows them to slowly but surely dismantle the house, one brick at a time.

The time is ripe and the ground is fertile to work the input of women into the soil and to see the fruits of their labor. It makes sense that church infrastructure would begin to reflect the ideas and styles of women leaders. No longer are women constrained to lead in male-defined ways. The church, therefore, no longer has to struggle with individualistic, top-down leadership that denies our claim to spiritual unity. We can and we have opted for change.

The Quest for Community and Unity

The forms of ministry in the church are named for us first in the book of Acts (2:42, 44-47). The word *ministry* is not used, but here one sees the Christian community doing what, in time, became the classical activities of ministry: *Kerygma*—proclaiming the word, preaching, evangelism; *Didache*—teaching; *Leiturgia*—coming together to pray and celebrate the eucharist; *Diakonia*—caring for those in need; *Koinonia*—community building, accountability. *Koinonia* has always been important for Christian spirituality; it is especially important today. At root it means sharing in something with someone—*part-*

nership. The Old Testament Hebrew precursor of this term is covenant, a binding together. The Pauline sense of it is Christocentric; salvation was *koinonia* with God, a corporate personality formed in Christ, the union of believers with Christ. Humans are saved not as isolated individuals but as members of God's people—not just a group, not just people who come together, but a unity. "So then you are no longer strangers and aliens, but you are citizens with the saints and also members of the household of God" (Eph. 2:19).

Faith is never in isolation. Jesus invited early followers not only to believe through a personal faith, but with a body through a shared faith. In the early church, according to Acts 5, the members even held all their possessions in common—if one suffered, all suffered; if one rejoiced, all rejoiced. In *Life Together*, Dietrich Bonhoeffer wrote, "Let him who cannot be alone beware of community. He will only do harm to himself and the community. . . . But the reverse is also true. Let him who is not in community beware of being alone. Into the community you were called."[8]

For many reasons this sense of real spiritual unity in community is rare. One factor is that our faith as a community is shaped by remembering, but few people know the particulars of their faith community's story. The Greek word for this kind of remembering is *anamnesis*, the opposite of amnesia. It is a cooperate memory: the memory of the story of God's people shaped by the life and death and resurrection of Jesus. Charles R. Foster laments the loss of cooperate memory in *Educating Congregations* and cites this loss as one of the signs and symptoms of church decline, as a flaw in the vessel of church education.[9]

The self-sacrifice and forgiveness needed to preserve *koinonia* counteract the self-promoting individualism and narcissistic introspection of current culture.

Relational leadership overcomes the trend toward "cocooning" and protecting ourselves from what is perceived as a harsh, cruel world. True community "sets us free for others." In Letty Russell's words, it "helps us to understand that the actual experience of leadership in Christian perspective is an exercise in partnership."[10]

Parker Palmer, well-known teacher and spiritual writer, wrote that institutions do not need leaders. They can survive by following their own bureaucratic rules, but community is dynamic and needs leadership at every turn—leadership from leaders who will call the community to its vision.[11] True community produces weblike leadership and web leadership produces true community. One reason for the lack of community is our frequent application of the mathematical symbol "is less than" to compare individuals in such statements as "this person is less than this person for this reason," or "that person is less than that person for this reason." Also, excessive conflict and a lack of love, flexibility, a giving spirit, and forgiveness work against community.

Often community is threatened when individuals who take initiative are accused of not working within the system. One woman on the staff of a church expressed her frustration at being told she was stepping out of bounds because she took the opportunity to help a nearby community service organization. The organization desperately needed food to distribute to those in need during the summer. She responded quickly to initiate a food drive in her church, involving as many people as possible; she talked with as many people as she could, mobilizing them to initiate more community food drives. Yet she was reprimanded for acting too quickly, not getting approval, not going through "proper channels," and not "coordinating" with everyone. To do this in the organizational structure of her church would have required that she wait a month for the appropriate committee to meet. Could it be that the problem was that it was a woman who took action? Was someone afraid of the attention she might get? Did others feel upstaged because she did the right thing and they did not? Do we have to get permission to help others? We do, of course, hold each other accountable, but God calls us into ministry and gives us all the permission we need.

In another example, a church educator planned and implemented a badly needed teacher-training event in her congregation and invited teachers from a neighboring church of the same denomination to join them. Anxious to begin the process, she worked with teachers who agreed with the need. A web of people were involved. One day she was called in by her CEO pastor, reprimanded, and put on probation because the male Christian education chairperson did not approve of her efforts. Because of his gender and position, he had been given implicit authority over this educator. The educator was unaware of the politics here and simply did what was necessary. She assumed because of her expertise in this area, and that because the church had hired her to do a job, she had been given the authority to do it. She assumed that the Christian education chairperson would support her in her efforts. She was told, "You work here for us." The feeling was that she had overstepped some invisible line of authority. Though some may argue that she was wrong in not going through the proper channels, we would argue, again, that one does not need permission to be in ministry. When something needs to be done, do it, but do it in a connectional way. That philosophy, unfortunately, will be punished in a hierarchial system.

We are painfully aware of the lack of community. Many feel anger toward the church because of its failure to deliver that promise of community. Still, there are some, like feminist theologian Letty Russell, who remain. Russell says that although she, like other alienated women, would sometimes like to walk away from the church, there is the recognition that the church is the bearer of the story of Jesus Christ and the good news of God's love. In addition, she says that the church needs some "uppity women and men." Why should we let the patriarchy drive us out?[12] As frustrating as the church may sometimes seem, it is richly endowed with God's blessings, and the Spirit is still present there! We are reminded of the poignant spiritual writing of Carlo Carretto, who captured the essence of our feelings toward the church:

> How baffling you are, oh Church, and yet how I love you!
>
> How you have made me suffer, and yet how much I owe you!
>
> I should like to see you destroyed, and yet I need your presence.
>
> You have given me so much scandal and yet you have made me understand sanctity.
>
> I have seen nothing in the world more devoted to obscurity, more compromised, more false, and I have touched nothing more pure, more generous, more beautiful. How often I have wanted to shut the doors of my soul in your face, and how often I have prayed to die in the safety of you arms.
>
> No, I cannot free myself from you, because I am you, although not completely.
>
> And where should I go?[13]

There still is a hungering for community, a longing to know and experience the joy of the Christian life lived in love, and we still have hope that it can be found in the church.

The Web as Matrix for Spiritual Unity

A Webster's dictionary defines a matrix as something that constitutes the place or point from which something else originates. The church today is a matrix of many theological influences and movements that shape beliefs and "bump into" one another. It is difficult to be in ministry and not be influenced by one or more theological orientations such as conservative, traditionalist, evangelical, feminist, liberationist, womanist, *mujerista* theology.

How might the matrix be uniting instead of divisive? Possibly by understanding that a matrix is also a mold, a frame with interconnecting rows and columns, and a weblike structure of organization. This matrix can create spiritual unity by interconnectedness instead of conflict and divisiveness. The matrix is held together by relationship and love. "Interdependency between women is a way to freedom which allows the *I* to *be*, not in order to be used, but in order to be creative."[14]

The assumption has been that the hierarchical structure was the way things were originally ordered, that it was ordained by God, that it was the way the church was intended to be. Before hierarchy (or at least alongside of it), however, there was another way of ordering things. The web matrix that we have been discussing is not a new image; but it is, in fact, recognized in some ancient cosmologies. Louv claims that the image of the circular, interconnected structure of social, psychological, and spiritual health appears in nearly every culture's mythology. He points out that the "prophet Isaiah, circa 730 B.C.E., wrote, 'There is One Who is dwelling above the circle of the earth, the dwellers of which are as grasshoppers, the One Who is stretching out the heavens just as a fine gauze, Who spreads them out like a tent in which to dwell.' "[15]

The sixth-century monk Dorotheus of Gaza imagined the world as a large circle with God in the middle. In this concept, human beings start their lives at the circle's edge. As they grow close to God, journeying toward the center of the circle, they also move closer to one another.

Black Elk, an Oglala Sioux holy man, described his vision of his nation as a weblike hoop, all encompassing and inclusive. In traditional African villages everything of importance takes place in a circle: meetings, worship, dances, eating, life in general.

The language of "headship" in the New Testament Pauline writings is in contrast with the original vision of the church at Pentecost, but this language set up a culturally induced and culturally perpetuated paradigm of patriarchal authority. The original notion of the church was not an exclusivist community, which is a distorted idea of community that was not in Jesus' teachings. Institutionalization brought about exclusion as a variety of Christian communities developed with widely differing interpretations of Jesus' message, each group believing that they were the sole bearers of the truth.

Now, more than ever, the web structure is evident in society. The web has become a powerful ecological metaphor as scientists no longer talk of the food chain, but the food web.[16] In these worldviews the overarching concept of the web was and is a powerful source of harmony and unity, as it might be for us. Living organisms are intertwined and interdependent. Biologists and environmentalists use the language of interconnectedness rather than the language of biological warfare or survival of the fittest. "Ecological studies offer a picture of nature less focused on the terrors of combat than on the dance of communal collaboration, a picture of the great web of being."[17]

Biblical Examples of Leadership for Spiritual Unity

There are many styles of leadership and organization represented in the Bible, some of them hierarchical, but upon closer examination, many are not. The Old Testament bears witness to the important role women played as leaders. Letty Russell points out that Miriam's leadership in exile exhibits a concern for the inclusion of people. Miriam is named by the prophet Micah (6:4). Although, in Numbers 12:2-14, she is rebuked and punished for criticizing Moses, she was not trying to take over so much as she was confronting patriarchal authority and the disregard of her people to advocate for a more inclusive form of leadership that serves and cares for the community.[18] This story exemplifies the tension between different types of authority and leadership, not God's preference for male, hierarchical leaders.

According to Judges 4:4, Deborah was a prophet who was serving as a judge for the Israelites. Though women were usually considered to be of a lesser status in the tradition, some female leadership emerged. Deborah is called the wife of Lappidoth, which means "woman of fire," and later is called a "mother in Israel" (5:7). Deborah served as a judge of all Israel. Her position was granted to her by divine appointment. There is no biblical discussion about Deborah's right to be a judge or whether she had to prove herself to others in order to gain their respect. Deborah, in Judges 4–5, had authority by title, office, function, and personal charisma. She broke the patriarchal mode.[19] She dispensed justice sitting under a palm tree in Ephraim, reaching out to people and doing her job using a nontraditional style of leadership. Exercising a "female advantage" in leadership, she placed herself at the center of her situation, not at the top in a hierarchical manner. She was accessible and based her decision making and judgments on conversations and ideas that flowed around her. Carol Lakey Hess says Deborah "inspires a vision of caretaking that is passionate, empathetic, and wise."[20] Extreme hierarchy in leadership, a hierarchy that the Hebrews rejected, had created sharp divisions among the Cannanites. From among them, Deborah emerged as a leader by common consent.[21] In short, the hierarchy was not working, so they sought leadership elsewhere.

The people did not constantly evaluate her perform-ance; they trusted her leadership as one called by God. They recognized that it was God's sovereign choice to empower her to leadership. Deborah did not need approval from top-down committees to give her permis-sion to make decisions. She articulated her wise judg-ments and implemented what was needed to get the job done. Not waiting for Barak to come to her, Deborah sent for him and issued the rallying cry to the people.

Ruth and Naomi were women leaders whose story is refreshing. Soon after Naomi and her husband moved from Bethlehem to the land of Moab, Elimelech died, leaving Naomi in a foreign land. When Naomi's two sons also died, her two Moabite daughters-in-law were faced with the decision of whether to remain with Naomi or return to their homes. Because Naomi is a for-eigner and a widow with no means of economic support, she plans to return to her home of Bethlehem. Orpah, following Naomi's suggestion decides to return to her home in Moab. Ruth decides to stay with Naomi:

> "Do not press me to leave you or to turn back from
>   following after you!
> Where you go, I will go; where you lodge, I will lodge;
>   your people shall be my people, and your God my God.
> Where you die, I will die—there will I be buried.
> May the LORD do thus and so to me,
>   and more as well,
> if even death parts me from you!" (Ruth 1:16-17)

This story is about the friendship between two women who are not competing against each other for status, power, or men. When thinking about these strong women who bind themselves together, we are compelled to remember that in spite of their diversity and their dif-ferent backgrounds, they stay together. No "angel of mercy" came to their defense, no authority told them what to do, and nothing legally bound them. These women depended on their strong faith that united them as "sister-friends." These women built a coalition with each other as equal partners. The younger one gleaned the fields, and the older one shared her wisdom and taught the younger one.[22] Stephen Rhodes sees this as a story about the risk of diversity. The women left Moab and moved to a new land. Naomi returned to her people, but Ruth, a Moabite, chose to stay with Naomi and live in a strange land. Still, Ruth was accepted among the Hebrews, which sends the message that "God's grace transcends and defies racial, religious, and national exclusiveness."[23]

The book of Esther provides two examples of weblike leadership. First, Queen Vashti, long considered to be unimportant to the story and virtually forgotten, refused male authority. She said "No." She refused to be paraded in front of a group of men to be stared at. Web leadership involves acts of defiance. Second, Esther, Mordecai's cousin who was chosen by King Ahasuerus as his next wife, provides an example. But Esther proved to be "more than just a pretty face," according to Katherine Pfisterer Darr.[24] Mordecai told Esther to keep her Jewish heritage to herself and not to tell her husband, and he revealed to her that there was a plot to assassinate her husband. The stage is set for Esther to do the needful thing. She interceded with the king on behalf of her people. Esther skillfully negotiates the power structure to attain her goal, the saving of her people.[25] She was flexible but stuck to her task, and she was relational in her mission. She connected with the diverse group of personalities that were around her. She did not use her position as Queen to force or command; she engaged in dialogue and hospitality. Her web of leadership was strong enough to have both "enemies" and friends at her banquet table. Her courage and her concern and care for her people took precedence over her personal considerations and concern for her status.

The unfolding story of Job reveals one who changes from a successful, self-satisfied head of the family to one who enters into dialogue with those around him and with God in an attempt to understand his suffering. In doing so, Job enters more fully into human community. No longer will he take people and blessings for granted. "In contrast to the lonely, rather controlling figure . . . in the beginning, we are met with a host who welcomes and entertains visitors by the end. Formerly complacent in his theology, now his own grappling with suffering has enabled him to see things from the perspective of others who suffer."[26] Web leadership developed as one leads from one's woundedness. Job cannot presume to know the sufferings and experiences of others and empathize with them until he himself has entered into that suffering and is marginalized.

A parable told by Jesus in Luke 18:1-8 is often cited to be about perseverance in prayer; a widow keeps returning to an unjust judge, who finally gives in so she would not continue to "wear me out." The most common interpretation of this parable focuses on the faithfulness of God in contrast to the unjust judge. But the truly wonderful thing about parables is the many doors and windows of insight into them. What makes this parable so shocking, so amazing, and so true is that this woman, this widow (a person of low status in that society), kept coming to the judge. She did not give up. She was persistent and that is what it took. She had to deal with the hierarchy, and as one person, she could not overthrow that judge. She was in a situation that she thought she could not change, but change it she did. We are ever grateful for the long line of female saints who kept coming and who carved out a path, though it still be rocky. The web leader seeks justice and does not give up. We have said that "the master's tools cannot be used to dismantle the master's house." In the interim, while the hierarchy still persists, we will have to keep at this task, continually coming to the authorities and pointing out injustice. This book is an example of such effort.

Prayer is a means of justice, and this parable demonstrates the strong relationship between prayer and a just order. If an unfair judge will give in to a widow, we can be assured that God will listen to and act on our prayers and pleas even more than the judge did for the widow.

Prayer is also a form of vindication. Through prayer, the community takes on a commitment to enact God's vision for the church. We pray continually for the church to more closely serve God's purpose, and we pray that we will be better able to align ourselves to that purpose and to implement change.

Perhaps the best example of such leadership in the Bible is in a description of the ministry of Jesus. His leadership reshaped human authority. He proclaimed, according to the Gospels, that the last shall be first. Jesus' ministry was a ministry to the margins. He included women in his circle of disciples. When Jesus first drew his followers together, he did not turn them inward to deal with their own needs. He sent them to treat the hurts of the spirit and body in the world around them. "In the community formed by Jesus, we are to be stretched continuously for others."[27] Jesus went to where the people were, to the "least of these," and they followed him. His message liberated them from bondage. The community he formed fed the hungry, welcomed the stranger, clothed the naked, cared for the sick, and visited the prisoner (Matt. 25:31-46). Jesus overturned the tables of the money changers, those in control of society. His was a ministry of healing and miracles, a ministry that stretched far beyond the geographic boundaries of his time and place. Jesus told stories of a better way and gave hope. He called together a small band of supporters and friends. He described himself as a vine with people as branches, creating a strong web of living, organic faith. He spoke of pursuing the lost sheep and going to the margins to do so and of welcoming the prodigal home.

The story of Jesus' encounter with the woman at the well in John 4 is a story of building community and crossing boundaries, according to biblical scholar Osvaldo Vena.[28] Jesus invited the Samaritan woman into dialogue as a true conversation partner. He crossed racial and gender barriers set up between a chosen and a rejected people. He did so by first becoming vulnerable, by asking for a drink of water and acknowledging that the woman had something that he needed, a bucket. The woman realizes that Jesus also has something that she needs—he is the giver of living water. This text tells us that community can only be built when people are not afraid to break social conventions. Jesus, too, was changed by the encounter. Initially Jesus voiced the opinion of Judaism in his day by criticizing Samaritans for not worshiping God in the accepted way . In reaching out to a despised people, Jesus learned that his ministry was not just to Jews but to everyone, and his own consciousness of his ministry expanded. This woman became a missionary, and "many Samaritans from that city believed in him because of the woman's testimony" (v. 39).

The story of Jesus feeding the five thousand in Mark 6:30-44 epitomizes web leadership. Jesus' feeling of compassion for the throng of people is evident in this story. Parker Palmer calls it a "compassionate *feeling with* other people."[29] The result is that a few provisions are somehow enough to satisfy a big crowd. This is not a tale of a magician who supernaturally makes food multiply.

What Jesus does instead of magic is to act on the assumption of abundance. First, he divides the crowd into "companies" of hundreds and fifties and commands them all "to sit down ... upon the green grass." His miracle begins with the simple act of gathering the faceless crowd of five thousand into smaller, face-to-face communities. This is the stock-in-trade of every good community organizer, this clustering of people into more intimate settings where everyday miracles have a chance to happen.[30]

When the people gathered into small groups they went from a nameless crowd into communities. They could no longer hoard their scarce resources. The text does not say that everyone went away full, it says they "all ate and were satisfied" (Mark 6:42 NIV). It is truly a miracle to have everyone in a group satisfied. The accepted wisdom in the church is "you can't please everyone." Our churches are filled with people who are dissatisfied, and they let us know it. They may be dissatisfied with the pastor, the Sunday school, the sermon, the color of the walls, the choice of hymns, whatever, but they do not give their time or their money. It is the culture of scarcity that creates and breeds dissatisfaction.[31]

Our refusal to believe that we have enough is one cause of the competition that has resulted in such an inequitable distribution of resources at home and around the world. But a culture of abundance both arises from and creates a sense of satisfaction. . . .

In the feeding of the five thousand, Jesus did not act alone and that is the key to his miracle. He acted in concert with others and evoked the abundance of community.[32]

Web leadership assumes such abundance in the diversity of community—the abundance of gifts given and multiplied by the Spirit.

With some exceptions, some of which we have described, there were three criteria for leadership and authority in ancient Israel: age, gender, and race. According to David Johnson and Jeff VanVonderen in *The Subtle Power of Spiritual Abuse,* you had to be old, you had to be male, and you had to be Hebrew. This was a good system for old Hebrew men. Jesus was the harbinger of change, and that change is evident in Acts 2 where spirit-filled men and women shared in leadership to bring forth the church.

The women in the early church were often the ones who demonstrated that function and service outweigh status and title in leadership. The widows described in the first epistle of Timothy, and other women named and unnamed, engaged in critical activities for the community: caregiving, hospitality, prayer, and making cloaks and distributing them. There was Tryphaena (Rom. 16:12) who shared in the work of evangelization. There was Prisca who shared the description "fellow worker in Christ Jesus" (Rom. 16:3) with her husband and accompanied Paul on a mission. Even though women were driven more to the periphery by the hierarchization of the church, they continued their "subversive" leadership and ministry.

Inclusiveness, God's Image, and the Body of Christ

The web as a matrix leading to spiritual unity begins with the *imago dei,* the image of God, as inclusive. When God finished creating us, male *and* female, in God's own image, God saw everything, according to Genesis, and proclaimed it good. All of creation is good and worthy. Gerrit Scott Dawson reminds us that "God does not exist in our image; we are made in God's image. God is neither male nor female. Rather God is all male is (and more) and all that female is (and more)."[33] God's own image is the basis of inclusivity. Of course, we are well aware of the long and twisted tale of the failure on our part and our attempts to divide and conquer and to rank and climb to the top. However, God remained and still remains attached to us. The original intention of *imago dei* remains intact.

To reflect God's image in the world we are called to be the church, gathered in the name of Christ and bonded together in love. According to M. Scott Peck:

> Community is and must be inclusive.
>
> The great enemy of community is exclusivity. Groups that exclude others because they are poor or doubters or divorced or sinners or of some different race or nationality are not communities; they are cliques—actually defensive bastions against community. . . .
>
> There is an "allness" to community. It is not merely a matter of including different sexes, races, and creeds. It is also inclusive of the full range of human emotions. Tears are as welcome as laughter, fear as well as faith.[34]

This interconnectedness is present in the scriptural metaphor of the Body of Christ. A surgically opened human body reveals the neat packaging of all the human organs inside the body. Each one has its own strong, healthy packaging or lining that separates it from the other organs. Flora Slosson Wuellner describes the value of the separate distinctiveness in accord with the unity of the bodily organs. Wuellner's message is that a bodily organ cannot be in healthy harmony and cooperation with the other organs unless it is distinctly separate.[35] The same is true within the Body of Christ as it is described in 1 Corinthians 12:12-27. Even though each body part has its own distinct task, all the parts need one another, and each one is lifted up and appreciated for who and what it is and does. This image affirms that God did not intend the church to define one universal, accepted, dominant method.

Healing in the Church

There has already been some healing of the broken-ness from disunity in the church, but there is still a long way to go. It will take time. Those of us who have been wounded are suspicious and doubtful of the church's efforts to reform. As a result, many more will leave. Some seek and find their sense of community outside the bounds of the Christian church. But as surely as God is faithful to the promises, there is hope for justice and healing. The stories of Jesus healing the sick reminds us not so much of the divine power of Jesus but of his love that brings about the compassionate mystery of healing. It follows, then, that much of web leadership involves healing, and as Henri Nouwen points out, those who are wounded become the healers and continue the spirit of Jesus' healing ministry. Connections need restoring and new relationships need to be made. While we have a long way to go, making these connections is a good place to start.

One of us attended a conference for deacons and dia-conal ministers in Houston, Texas, in October of 1998. One worship service for this conference was highly unusual. It was a funeral—a funeral for the church; there was even a coffin. At first, participants were leery. Were we doing something blasphemous here? The somber mood of the liturgy touched our pain and began to move us. We committed the hierarchical way of thinking that is entrenched in the church to burial. We committed the racism and sexism perpetuated by the church "to the earth."

Autopoesis is a word from the field of biological engi-neering describing the will to live. This phenomenon is present in all living things and represents noble efforts to stay alive. While *autopoesis* is a positive gift, it can also be a bane to our existence. Life is meant to be a cycle of birth and death. When something refuses to die and give itself up to necessary change and transformation, that refusal is, in fact, destructive. There are some ways of doing things in the church that are ready to die, and we must let them. The funeral in Houston acknowledged the death of many of these things; now we need to bury them. It was also a funeral to say good-bye to jealousy, positional power, and territorialism. A funeral can be a healing experience, a time to lay something to rest, and a time to celebrate a new life, a transformed life. In Houston, the end of the funeral was a jazz recessional with those present dancing in the aisles to the music of "When the Saints Go Marching In" and expressing hope for a new life for the church. We are, in the words of the poet Julia Esquivel, "threatened with the resurrection."

> Join us in this vigil
> and you will know what it is to dream!
> Then you will then know how marvelous it is
> to live threatened with Resurrection![36]

New Understandings of Faith Community

To restore the intended spiritual unity of the Body of Christ, we return to the weblike matrix with which we started. It is clear that the effects of increased diversity demand a new way of leading that is inclusive. The matrix of the web gives rise to leadership that transcends theological orientations, race, and gender. A web style of leadership allows spiritual unity to evolve, almost piece-meal, rather than result from some grand design conceived and carried out by only a few persons. According to Sally Helgesen, webs are often instituted in response to some specific organizational crisis where there is little time to develop detailed blueprints or long-range strategic plans. What this means is that leaders discover what works and does not work as they go along. Does this diminish the role of preparation for ministry? No, it just calls for a different kind of preparation—one that does not give prescribed answers to certain "cases" but prepares people to manage a crisis, to look for new solutions, and to take risks.

A web style of leadership will have more voice and credibility in diverse communities than the old hierarchical styles of leadership will. It requires a change in the position of leadership—from the "top" to the "center"—not simply because this is a preferred way of female leadership, but because it is expedient and called for today. The CEO-style senior pastor is not thriving. There is visible evidence of a decline among churches where the pastor is a CEO. In hierarchical leadership, we can burn out too early because we often believe that everything is in our hands, and not infrequently, there is an abuse of top-down power that brings about litigation and creates the worse kind of divisiveness and failure in a church.

When we use the web image or web leadership style, we can still maintain our professional space as "organs" in the Body of Christ. Interdependence is not codependence—the creation of an "everything depends and hinges on me" attitude. None of Christ's teachings encourage codependence among his followers. We are diverse, and we are opposites, but we are connected by our love in Jesus Christ. We believe that Jesus is pleased when we eat, play, work, serve, and rest together in his name—while remaining unique in our identities.

In a web style of leadership, we are not in a mechanical relationship that makes us function as a conduit or an electric wire that is attached to Christ. Instead, we are in an organic relationship, a holographic relationship, in which the whole is encoded and inherent in each of the parts.[37] Using the web style of leadership, we can experience being connected and sharing without self-shredding.

Our human abilities, work, and ministries are gifts from a God who loves each of us.

Grace Gifts

Can you imagine a local church with people who are not separated or divided by categories that define their identity, such as pastors, staff, and laypeople? Is it possible to create a specific leadership pattern for a body with many members, all with gifts interdependent on one another, in a ministry in which members of the body lead with the gifts that God has given to them. In a system like this, Jesus is at the center and at the margins. Jesus is the source, and it is his Spirit we rely on to meet needs, not the pastor. When God is depended on to meet needs and all the people are resources, no one person is ahead of another. In 1 Corinthians 12:11-12 and 18, Paul wrote:

> But one and the same Spirit works all these things, distributing to each one individually just as He wills.
>
> For even as the body is one and yet has many members, and all the members of the body, though they are many, are one body, so also is Christ.
>
> But now God has placed the members, each one of them, in the body, just as He desired. (NASB)

This organizational structure is very different from our unhealthy system of leadership where the people focus on the pastor or paid staff to meet their needs.

One way to adjust our churches and to restore their effectiveness for unity is to discover and use the resources of the people or "grace gifts" or spirit gifts. A priesthood common to all does not mean there is no diversity of gifts. The Body of Christ, the faith community, would be built up by leading according to God's gifting rather than by human ordering.[38] Weblike leadership understands and affirms the Christian vocation of all baptized persons. Despite all the talk about how we all share in the one ministry of Jesus Christ, many Christians are still unaware of the fact that God has gifted them for ministry. Their light has been held "under a bushel." As web-style leaders, we could help people see and claim their giftedness then "get out of the way" so they could be in ministry. We would speak of people being in ministry rather than being lay volunteers and write "spirit" descriptions rather than job descriptions.

One caution is in order, however, as Robin Maas points out in *Crucified Love*. The quest for understanding one's gifts can be a quest for self-fulfillment instead of a quest to serve God. "It is a bit like peeling away the layers of an onion," she says, "in an attempt to get to an inner core.... Those of us who peel and chop onions have learned that there is no 'core' to speak of, just layer after layer."[39] So the quest for discovery of spiritual gifts is not a quest for personal authenticity but a quest for wholeness and holiness.

According to Helgesen, weblike leadership emphasizes process as well as structure because it establishes new ways of approaching problems, thinking, connecting people, giving information, and motivating people.[40] In ministry this means recognizing each person's unique grace gifts without pressing false limits upon them (such as, you can't do this or that because ...). Everyone is included and contributes something in the decision-making process.

Technology: A Two-Edged Sword

Today's technology makes the divisions between thinking and doing obsolete because those who want access to information and expertise can get it, and they can make strategic decisions based on that information and expertise. Technology is creating a world of equal access. This helps those on "the bottom." There are no secrets. Because of computers, the globe is shrinking.

The world is getting smaller, and people are more connected. However, in spite of technology's ability to link people together across the globe, technology can also isolate people and prevent them from forming community with those nearby. It is now possible to shop, bank, seek medical advice, pursue academic degrees, and engage in countless other activities without ever leaving the house or seeing another person. As Leonard Sweet has observed, postmodern technology is almost alive with computers writing their own software and people flying on airplanes controlled by computers rather than people.[41] The danger of dehumanization and mechanistic control is real. Overcoming this hazard is a challenge that may be met head-on in web leadership, with its insistence on interaction and its steadfast refusal to give up on community.

Web leadership can further expand the possibilities for connectedness through technology. The Internet is changing the way some churches are in ministry with their congregations and community. Ministry on the Internet expands the reach of local churches and is becoming more commonplace. These churches can disseminate information and connect people to one another, providing spiritual nourishment as well. Churches can connect with seminaries, making each church a "virtual seminary," further blurring the line between the trained and the untrained. Using phone lines and satellites, churches have access to multilevel, interactive distance learning via video conferencing. Faith communities, formerly perceived as bound together in love within a given geographical location, are no longer limited by their geography. With the technology to "get people together," there is immense opportunity for unity, but the opportunity is undergirded by a great responsibility to use technology for the glory of God and not for self-serving purposes.

Creating Space

In web leadership creating space is critical. The open spaces are where ministry happens, where people meet, greet, and take stock. It is where we minister by "walking around," because walking around is how we get to the margins. It is also how people at the margins can find their space in the community.

Several of the web leaders described by Sally Helgesen design office space so they can be at the center of things rather than holed up in some lofty, secluded "ivory tower" called an office. If they have quiet study that needs to be done, they do it someplace else. Like ideas, the working space is shared, and people do not venture off into their own little cubicle worlds or corner offices. Harrison Owen, mentioned in chapter 1, is the creator of Open Space Technology, which is a simple approach to a structure for getting things done. He found that often at conferences the most exciting conversations took place during the coffee breaks. The open space method simply brings people together in a circle without hierarchical constraints. He claims that when an inconspicuous facilitator creates or opens up the space and holds the space and keeps its sanctity amazing things take place—complex projects are born and deeply conflicted groups find commonality.[42]

In the work of the church the same applies. As the true work of the church, the liturgy needs open space with the community gathered around. Letty Russell describes such a church in East Harlem. The church took out the rows of pews to create a large space in the center in which a round table was added; the community gathered around this table to worship.[43] The round table, a symbol of hospitality in many cultures became a metaphor for the ministry there. Similarly, a church in Washington, D.C., has no anchored pews and celebrates eucharist-in-the-round rather than theater style, offering a rich image of its sacramental theology. At another church the people form a circle around the outer walls and celebrants move around with the people serving the elements to one another—no more passive sitting and waiting for the priest to feed me. Little attention is focused on one or two leaders, and great attention is given to "the priesthood of all believers." The circular, web-like communion service embodies the unity implied in the scripture: "For we being many are one bread, and one body; for we are all partakers of that one bread" (1 Cor. 10:17 KJV).

It is, indeed, a challenge to bring about such reconceptualization and change in the church. Though the web image has been around for many years and is relatively easy to understand and carry out, it will take more than a few "web leaders" to effect real change. Still, we are optimistic because when we describe web leadership, many people tell us that is how they lead or at least how they would like to lead. Web leadership is a grassroots movement that must evolve and come into its own. We believe, however, that it can and must be done. Who knows? Maybe we were raised up for just such a time as this.

A Prayer for the Church

Gracious God, we pray for your Holy Church. We know the night is very dark, but we remember that "only when it's dark enough, can you see the stars." Wondrous God, we come to you with outstretched arms, open eyes, and empty hands. We know we have created a church where persons are despised for the color of their skin, the language they speak, the gender they exhibit, the beliefs they possess, and the persons they choose to love. We wrap our hatred in scripture, doctrine, polity, and inclusive language hoping you will not notice. Forgive us, O God, for being fools for

71

the sake of the world instead of for you. O God, who reconciled the world through Christ Jesus, open the minds and hearts of an unwilling church to see a new creation and live as the people of the new Jerusalem. Amen.

CHAPTER THREE

The Web and Diversity

Diversity really means being able to draw from a wider base of talent.

SALLY HELGESEN, *THE WEB OF INCLUSION*

It is not those differences between us [of race, age, and sex] that are separating us. It is rather our refusal to recognize those differences, and to examine the distortions which result from our misnaming them and their effects upon human behavior and expectation.

AUDRE LORDE, *SISTER OUTSIDER*

If the church does not change, it may well have paid the final installment on its worst nightmare.

FUMITAKA MATSUOKA, *THE COLOR OF FAITH*

This chapter is, in actuality, a continuation of the previous one. Spiritual unity, we will argue here, *is* diversity. Unity in diversity has become almost a cliché, yet unity still eludes us. Diversity, we believe, is not about numbers nor is it a politically correct buzzword; it is a state of being, an attitude, and a way of life. The issue of diversity is not new to the church. The church has always struggled with "otherness," and one of the primary concerns of Paul was "the management of diversity, so that it does not become divisive."[1] Acts 2 is the story of how the "Holy Spirit descended upon the cacophonous

73

humanity gathered in Jerusalem" and transformed their "dissonant voices into holy harmony."[2] Pentecost is a model for what should be. Individuals who had been separated by their differences of race, culture, and language could now, with the influx of the Spirit, understand one another. The sign of the presence of the Spirit was not so much the speaking in tongues but the breaking down of the racial and cultural barriers between people.[3] One of the most prominent, perennial concerns of the church is for the faithful to find unity or communion in our differences.[4]

Diversity is not just differences of race, religion, gender, sexual orientation, culture, or age, but it is the differences in the way we think and act, differences in knowing (epistemology), ability, and interpretation. It encompasses all the ways that people differ.[5] It is important to note that cultural diversity, where persons of various cultures exist alongside each other, is a fact of human existence. Yet, more and more, anthropologists tell us that society is not simply a collection of varied and culturally well-defined groups. The lines are not drawn so clearly anymore. It is inadequate to define individuals and social groups in binary terms—delimiting persons, for example, as either black or white, gay or straight. The identities of these groups are more fluid. Assuming that everyone can or wants to place themselves in one racial category or another can be dehumanizing. Most individuals are a mix of ethnic identities and heritages.

In the microcosm of the church, this realization of diversity is rarer because the congregations tend to be homogeneous. There are, however, a growing number of congregations that embrace diversity, even striving to become *multicultural*, so that one culture is not dominant. These communities see themselves as being more than one entity or serving more than one function at a time and working to affirm equity in the power relations of the various cultural groups.[6] Use of the term *multicultural*, however, is hindered by the varying ideologies associated with it. The term *embrace* has been adopted by some to represent the goal of moving toward unity in diversity. Rather than just existing together or tolerating one another, individuals who are different from one another begin to embrace one another. The sheer act of embracing resembles weblike behavior. The arms encircle and invite the other to reciprocate. The movement of the self to the other and back is a cyclical one.

Still, for the most part, even as we "deal" with living with a multitude of cultures today, we have not even finished the business of mastering black and white relations or male and female relations, despite the impact of the civil rights and feminist movements. With the exceptions noted above, most Protestant congregations remain homogeneous and segregated. According to Miroslav Volf, "Churches, the presumed agents of reconciliation, are at best impotent and at worst accomplices in the strife."[7]

Yet theologically, at least, Christians look for a way of relating to one another that is based on something other than the idea that differences and opposition determine our identity.[8] Our differences are what allow us to forge relationships and spin ties. Otherwise we are a series of dots like a child's dot-to-dot picture that has not been completed. The Christian tradition has a strong mandate for hospitality toward the alien, the stranger, the "other." The scripture does not say, "Find out if a certain person meets all your criteria; then, if so, offer them hospitality." It tells us to make room for the stranger, the alien in our midst.

Some new diversity initiatives in society and the church attempt to eradicate oppression in all forms and in all areas. One goal, adapted from *Teaching for Diversity and Social Justice* by Adams, Bell, and Griffin, is the aim for full and equal participation of all groups in church and society. This vision is one in which the distribution of resources, both material and otherwise, is equitable, and all members are physically, psychologically, and spiritually safe.

Barriers to "Embracing Diversity"

An orchid is a beautiful flower; its beauty is enhanced by its diversity, a gradation of color and design. In raising orchids, creating conditions in which they can thrive is a challenge—just as creating conditions for ministry to bloom and thrive in diversity is a challenge. Letty Russell claims that differences are "God-given actions of creation" that "lend excitement to this world."[9] Nevertheless, one huge barrier to unity is that *differences threaten us*. Differences are allowed to create suspicion and threaten our way of life, resulting in a fear known as xenophobia. One such construct of difference—race—may have been an invention of European cultures that served political purposes and needs for territorial domination.[10] Race is a socially constructed notion that divides people, artificially, into distinct groups based on physical characteristics such as skin color. Many of the sins we commit against our neighbor are called sins of "exclusion" by Miroslav Volf in *Exclusion and Embrace: A Theological Exploration of Identity, Otherness, and Reconciliation*. In extreme cases we kill people and drive them out. This is exclusion as elimination. The cultural "cleansings" that have dominated the news in the past decade are the result of exclusion and the failure to embrace.[11] If in America, we think, smugly, that the atrocities that happened in Rwanda, Bosnia, and Kosovo could "never happen here," we have to remind ourselves of the offense of slavery—an accepted practice for three hundred years in this country—and the abuses of the indigenous peoples as they were driven from their rightful homelands. The roots of the poison ivy of racism are still fertile.

One of the deepest fears of being human is "of having a live encounter with alien 'otherness.' "[12] That fear is exploited in countless films, such as *Alien*, *Independence Day*, and *Men in Black*, that are produced in Hollywood and elsewhere. A few scattered films such as *E.T.* and the *Star Wars* series project the aliens as more endearing, causing viewers to like them in spite of their "ugliness." The fear of a live encounter with the "other" is the fear of diversity.

> As long as we inhabit a universe made homogeneous by our refusal to admit otherness, we can maintain the illusion that we possess the truth about ourselves and the world—after all, there is no "other" to challenge us! But as soon as we admit pluralism, we are forced to admit that ours is not the only standpoint, the only experience, the only way, and the truths we have built our lives on begin to feel fragile.[13]

There will be a certain amount of friction as individuals who are different bump against each other. What is truly miraculous, though, is how it is often possible to work together in creative synergy in spite of our various theologies, codes, and belief systems. We can learn to articulate our differences and find acceptable ways to talk about the insights gained from each other in these friction-producing situations.[14]

The church is no stranger to the politics of exclusion. A woman who served on the staff of a church in Christian education was fired. There was no warning, no due process. She was never given a reason for the termination, but she believes it was because she was doing "too good of a job." The Christian education ministry was on fire. Dozens of new small groups were forming. Attendance in classes and groups exceeded attendance in prior years. Christian education was getting too much attention and outshining other ministries. The church spent more money attempting to defend the firing than the educator was paid in a year. The rejection of diversity is reflected in the unequal distribution of resources, in little things like allocation of furniture and parking, and, more significantly, in practices like personnel policies. Some churches in "employment at will" states have, in fact, adopted employment at will clauses in keeping with the laws of their states, which employees are required to sign if they want a job.

An employment at will state is a state that permits employers to fire someone without giving a reason or any notice. This policy creates an imbalance of power between the employer and the employee—with the employer having nearly total control over the employee's future. For example, a volatile employer could fire someone on whim. Some churches in these states have incorporated the state's employment at will policy into their own personnel policy. Even though employees can also choose to leave their jobs at will, the employee depends on the employer for a job and, as a result, is forced to sign a form that says he or she accepts the employment at will clause—understanding that she or he could be fired at any time and giving away most of his or her rights.

We believe that in a church the relationship between employer and employee can be more of a covenant relationship. Only in extreme circumstances should a church fire someone without two weeks notice. If, for example, an employee has committed a serious crime, the termination could be immediate but with two weeks severance pay. In most circumstances, provision for appropriate counseling should be made for the employee. Another valuable technique is a termination interview for the employee with a personnel advocacy committee or a skilled human resources consultant; such an interview can ease the transition for both parties and help prevent future employment mistakes. Conversely, an employee also has covenantal responsibilities and therefore cannot walk out with no regard to the consequences for others.

There are theological problems with the legalistic approach that some churches take with their employees. The church has to stand against society as a community against unfair practices. "Our coziness with the surrounding culture has made us so blind to many of its evils that, instead of calling them into question, we offer our own versions of them—in God's name and with a good conscience."[15]

Another form of that exclusion is abandonment, seen most commonly in the United States as "white flight." It is "crossing over to the other side of the road," bystanding, keeping our distance so that the pain of others does not affect us. "Indifference can be more deadly than hate."[16] Because the differences threaten us, we have created a "hierarchy of cultures" that permeates our society and our churches and allows us to keep our distance.[17] *Hierarchical leadership* is another barrier that pushes those of low status to the bottom (or the margins). Difference is used to "stack" or rank people. Difference is used to define and distribute privilege. Some examples of privilege that many people from dominant groups take for granted are provided by the American Association of University Women's *Diversity Tool Kit*. As a result of being white, straight, able-bodied, and male, you can:

- browse in a store without being followed,
- hold your partner's hand in public,
- go in the front door even if there are stairs,
- attend a military academy without being harassed.

Privilege is an "invisible, weightless knapsack of special provisions, maps, passports, code books, visas, clothes, tools, and blank checks."[18]

Economics also plays a factor in the ranking, and cultures, which seem to "make it" and achieve success in the white-dominated society rank higher. The ranking applies not only to race and culture, however, but to just about any difference. These acts of subordination make prolific use of the mathematical "is less than" symbol (mentioned in chapter 1). For example, the unspoken rules of local church life are sometimes:

- Your call *is less than* mine because your call is not to the pastoral ministry;
- You *are less than* me because I'm ordained and you are not;
- You *are less than* me because I'm an elder and you're a deacon;
- You *are less than* me because I'm a pastor and you're an educator;
- You *are less* credible than I am as a boss because I have a credential that you don't have.

Ranking serves to divide and conquer. If we do not rank, we "tokenize" ("OK, we'll let you in as the one woman or black or Hispanic of our staff"). Under tokenism, it may be permissible, or even advisable, for a white congregation to have a few blacks, a few Asians, and perhaps a sprinkling of Hispanics while maintaining a "don't ask, don't tell" policy toward gays and lesbians. Some new churches or communities—African American, Korean, or gay congregations—for example, have been formed in order to preserve a sense of identity as a minority culture. These constituencies are responding to their exclusion by predominantly straight or white congregations who have often perceived them as threatening. The question raised by dividing churches into separate, culturally or ethnically centered entities is, How can we preserve and celebrate differences and self-identity while not giving up on the idea of Pentecost or unity in the Spirit? "The dynamics of difference need not be threatening, but instead contribute to enriched views."[19]

A hierarchy tries to build community by *assimilation*—by eliminating diversity. Assimilation can create another barrier—*the myth of uniformity and conformity*. Do the words uttered by Rodney King, "Can't we all just get along?" mean we accept our differences and embrace one another, or do they mean that the powerless had better succumb to the powerful for their own good? This very barrier might be the weight that tips the scales against the church. The church may be failing because diversity, which it refuses to accept, just is—it cannot be eliminated. Attempts can be made to maintain a fortress that is separate from society and practices its own traditions, but that is not church as we believe and know it is supposed to be. Hierarchy and diversity are mutually incompatible. According to Letty Russell, we have come to accept a deformed "pseudo-community"; "we have been taught by patriarchal structures of domination that community means sameness, uniformity and control."[20]

Community is not a "warm cozy feeling produced by sameness."[21] Unity does not mean uniformity, and as we discussed in the last chapter, it is contrary to think that we can create community without diversity. Too often the approach of congregations is "we welcome everybody" or "we are color blind." Sometimes these congregations even sincerely desire a more diverse membership but are unwilling or unable to make the sacrifices they need to make in order to meet this goal. Too often something like, "our doors are open to all" really means "we welcome you to become like us, to adopt our culture, our worship style, and our leadership style." *Assimilation* is a more benign form of exclusion than elimination, but no less dangerous to the Christian church.[22] Self-absolution, or making one's own group or culture absolute creates isolation and the dissolution of humanity.[23] The misappropriation and misunderstanding of the idea of God's chosen people has been an excuse for exclusion and racism.[24] The melting pot metaphor in reference to the United States is the dominant culture saying to everybody else, Come on and blend in. "At the same time, whenever the church consciously or unconsciously caters exclusively to one race or class, it loses the spiritual force of the 'welcoming each other' posture and is in danger of becoming little more than 'a social club with a thin veneer of religiosity.' "[25] To base our togetherness on what we have in common and ignore our differences is an incomplete picture. It is our differences that make us a community.

Korean theologian Kim Yong Bok describes solidarity as a chain, each link vital to the power of the whole. In some minority cultures, the chain is a powerfully negative metaphor. As a symbol of solidarity, however, the chain is a postmodern metaphor for being and acting together. To engage in an act of solidarity does not require sameness or unity. Partners in solidarity respect and in fact celebrate one another's distinctiveness as they take a stand against a commonly perceived oppression or injustice or as they work together for some common good. The shift from unity in diversity to solidarity is a theological shift according to Greer Anne Wenh-In Ng.[26] Solidarity also presupposes action—usually an action of resistance. It implies an element of risk. Solidarity can become oppressive itself when it is forced on someone or on some group, perhaps by those who want to feel generous or who want to salve their conscience or satisfy their need to be good Samaritans. True solidarity is possible when mutuality exists, when the motivation is justice rather than charity, and when the participating groups or persons have equal power and status. Solidarity allows the oppressed to choose the margins as a place of resistance, and it prevents the center from absorbing the margins, from assimilating the marginalized into its culture.[27]

The authors of *Teaching for Diversity and Social Justice* provide a good summary of the defining features of oppression. These ideas resonate with what we know and have experienced both in the secular world and in the church. Oppression, according to the authors, is pervasive. It is seen in all areas of social discourse; it is woven through society. Many cultural influences contribute to the oppression of ethnic groups. Although the presence of minorities is increasing in positions of power, we are still socialized by the idealizing of powerful white role models, such as the president of the United States, judges, members of Congress, and television personalities, and by holding up whiteness as a standard of normality in smaller matters, such as thoughtless terminology like the designation of "flesh" as a color for crayons and "nude" as a color of women's pantyhose.[28] Social inequality is not in isolated pockets but is pervasive and ingrained. Therefore, the denominational church cannot escape it. Oppression is also restrictive. It restricts certain people from full participation and affects their opportunity and hopefulness. The church, the Body of Christ, certainly restricts many people from full participation (as we have discussed), relegating numerous individuals to the periphery.

Next, oppression is hierarchical. Oppression signifies a hierarchical relationship in which dominant or privileged groups benefit, often in unconscious ways, from the disempowerment of a subordinated (target) group. And inversely, hierarchy, wherever it exists—especially in the church!—signifies oppression. Oppression is internalized. It resides not only in external social institutions, but oppressive beliefs also become a part of the human psyche, of both the victims and the oppressors. The idea that the poor may somehow deserve or are responsible for their own poverty is a misconception that is sometimes held by the poor and the affluent alike. Hegemony is the claim to supremacy by a dominant group that projects a perspective so successfully that it is accepted by everyone as part of the natural order, even those on the bottom. This acceptance is what Paulo Freire called the oppressed playing host to the oppressor.[29]

Internalized acceptance of the status quo can lead subordinated people to turn against members of their own group who challenge it. Despite the general endorsement of the notion, "that's just the way things are," God's intention for creation has always been multicultural. The blessing of God was that the descendants of Abraham should multiply and that nations should be built and spread throughout the earth. The story of the Tower of Babel signifies the beginning of the end of unity in diversity. In an attempt to preserve themselves—fearing they would be scattered—and to survive by their own means instead of relying on God, the people built a tower, a fortress. The result of this was dissonance and confusion, babbling and lack of understanding.[30] Perhaps church hierarchy is a modern day Tower of Babel. In our need for self-preservation we have built a structure in which we attempt to govern ourselves with rules and norms, often without relying on God. The "tower" serves to isolate and insulate us from the world and confuse our speech.

Finally, oppression is interconnected.[31] One form of oppression leads to another. This is what is meant by the web of oppression, using the metaphor in its negative sense. Oppression of one group affects all groups. It does no good to try to ascertain which group is the most oppressed in America. The subordination of any group undermines God's vision of the church. We can work to dismantle the web of oppression and replace it with a web of unity.

Diversity in Leadership

How important are gender, cultural, and ethnic differences in leadership in the church? Are gender differences more significant than those based on race or age or place of origin? No one knows the answer to this question, but most sociologists agree that these identities of gender, culture, and ethnicity profoundly shape how we act, what we do, and how we do it. Certainly gender does make a difference and women's leadership has profoundly influenced the church in this century. It was not many years ago that "the man in the long black robe" was the only model for ministry in the church. Women were told they could not or should not be pastors or ministers. A generation that grows up today sees and experiences very different leadership in the church. Most of this generation do not question the presence of women in the pulpit or can even imagine a time when women were absent from leadership.

For some, acknowledging that women are different and do things differently jeopardizes the concept of equality because it implies that women are weak and cannot keep up. Some analyses of women's development and gender differences have been criticized for stereotyping women as being softer or more caring than men. The desire to affirm that women are up to the task of leadership sometimes carries with it a reluctance to admit such gender differences, according to sociolinguist Deborah Tannen, because differences can be used to deny opportunity. Tannen's and others' research, however, indicate that gender differences are evident in the ways we act and in the way we communicate and that we need to identify and understand them.[32] The criticism of acknowledging gender differences buys into the notion that women have to be like "one of the boys." Carol Becker considers this pure nonsense. It is true, however, that women working in a patriarchal organization like the church often do conform to the styles of their male colleagues in order to survive or get ahead because hierarchy stifles diversity. The hierarchy blinds people from seeing the value of different styles of leadership.[33]

Sally Purvis, in *The Stained Glass Ceiling*, addressed the question regarding the effect women clergy have in parishes by studying two female pastors in Atlanta, Georgia—one Presbyterian and one Episcopalian. She found that their work was characterized as a process of clearing or chipping away the "residue of resentment" toward women in ministry and the reservations about their leadership ability. Based on her study of these two women, Purvis concluded that there was no "woman's way of leadership." We would agree that there is no single female style. Yet she did find there were differing expectations and that the women's leadership did make a difference in their congregations. Purvis alluded to the fact that changes took place in the congregations because the pastors were women—changes that might not have been made by male pastors or, at least, had not been made by their male predecessors. One of the most apparent modifications was the redesigning of worship space in one of the churches. The woman pastor eliminated the congregation's traditional practice of the priest celebrating the Eucharist with "his" back to the congregation. Another change was the expansion of the congregation's inclusivity and involvement in social justice issues. Even though these two women chose to avoid challenging hierarchy and to lead in traditional ways, not stressing gender, Purvis described the leadership style of the female pastors as strong, nurturing, motherly, and family and children oriented.[34]

Silent Barrenness

The hierarchy, in its inability to contend with diversity, has a way of silencing people. Deborah Shepherd compares women moving into leadership to immigrants entering a new culture.[35] They are quiet because they do not speak the language. Women and other marginalized groups have been reduced to silence and invisibility for years. "Communion is not possible where speech is destroyed by callousness, violence, and other acts that erode trust among people."[36] Rebecca Chopp, in *The Power to Speak*, describes the experience of women as being "forever strangers" to the dominant (not necessarily the majority) group in the congregation and to the need to find a voice in order to help "revise the social and symbolic rules of language" that govern the institution.[37]

The silence is not so much from not being capable of good speech, but more from a desire to survive. We have seen the dynamics of how this "silencing" works. In a recent planning meeting for a large regional church event, we observed a general brainstorming of ideas for the program. Most of those at the meeting were pastors. One woman, a youth minister, voiced an idea. One of the male pastors immediately made a sarcastic remark, putting down her idea, and yes, he got a good laugh from the committee. A little while later this woman expressed another idea. In violation of the ground rules of good brainstorming, the same male pastor jumped in with a dismissive, "that doesn't float my boat, and besides it won't work." A couple of us made feeble attempts to affirm her but realized that we came across as attempting to rescue her. This woman did not say another word at that meeting and dropped out of the committee. The male pastor seemed to have some stake in making sure only his ideas or those of his male colleagues were accepted, as if it were a matter of personal pride. By critiquing other ideas that were expressed, he ensured that only his ideas were left.

We are not saying that silencing is only a male behavior. In hierarchical situations silencing can be practiced by anyone in power. A well-respected seminary professor and feminist scholar argued persuasively for a particular interpretation of a passage of scripture. A Korean student tentatively raised his hand. The professor ignored him, but he was persistent, keeping his hand up for five minutes. Finally the professor called on the student, but it was as if he was bothering her. As the student tried to articulate his question, the professor was visibly annoyed. The answer was a muted version of, That's not a legitimate question, it has nothing to do with what I'm saying.

In chapter 1 we alluded to the studies that indicate the attrition rates of women in ministry. The United Methodist Clergywomen Retention Study conducted by Elizabeth J. Collier at the Anna Howard Shaw Center at Boston University School of Theology refers to "the oppressive silence of the promising, bright voices" and to the gifts and graces that the church is "losing out on because of its fear of change." This study surveyed 2,796 current and former clergywomen and interviewed 123 women to attempt to learn why large numbers of clergywomen who had intended to serve a local church were not doing so. The women were pastoring under the United Methodist itinerant system that "guarantees" an appointment to persons ordained elder. A significant percentage of those who left local church ministry said they left because "they believed they could not maintain their integrity in the system."[38] A greater extent of ethnic minority women (particularly African American and

Asian women) have left local church ministry than have white women.[39]

This study identified five areas or factors in the reasons women have left or are leaving local church ministry. One was frustration with or distrustfulness toward the appointment system. These women felt they were not getting the best appointments. There is an implicit glass ceiling. Also, family responsibilities were not taken into consideration. Having children was viewed as a detriment to the pastoral ministry for women in some cases. Another factor was the hierarchical leadership and lack of collegiality in the competition for appointments. One woman reported that bishops and cabinets refuse to appoint a black or a woman to some churches in some towns on the grounds that "they wouldn't be accepted." In the guise of protecting them, those who make the decisions about appointments were excluding African Americans or women or others. They were allowing the churches to discriminate in negotiating appointments.[40] Another reason given for leaving was the lack of acceptance by congregations and problems that cultural and gender differences engender.[41] Despite the now well-established presence of women in ministry, some women still encounter resistance to their leadership and the ways in which they lead. The reception of women in ministry varies greatly within the church. Southern and Midwestern states are notoriously resistant to the ministry of women, according to the C-4 study of The United Methodist Church. The following statements from personal interviews conducted with women in ministry were typical responses:

When I was serving a church, it seemed like everything I did was wrong. They were hypercritical. It wasn't like I went in and changed a lot of things either.

I love the ministry. I've had to learn to live with the negative stuff, though. It is worth it to fulfill my call.

Pastoring that church was bad for my spirit and self-esteem. I wasn't prepared to fight with them.

In the "system" it is just easier to get a pastor moved than it is to deal with differences and meet with conflict head-on.

Pastors have to climb a pyramid of appointments, and the sense is that only by "paying one's dues" can you move up.

My style of leadership and understanding of ministry was very different from what they were used to. They thought I should just be busy all the time and do everything. When I tried to involve them or ask for their help, they said no. The sense was, That's what we're paying you to do. It has taken about four years to make any progress.

Many of the women indicated that seminary did not prepare them for the local church or for the sexism they might experience there. Last, the clergywomen indicated they bear some of the responsibility themselves. Their lack of self-care and failure to find a support system were factors in many decisions to leave. Each of these factors is a silencing of these "bright voices."

Frederick W. Schmidt recounts a similar situation in the Episcopal Church. Although women have begun to attend seminaries in record numbers, he says, women continue to serve churches in smaller numbers than men and are locked out of most positions of significant leadership. There is a mistaken assumption that women have succeeded in the church, but Schmidt asserts that the Episcopal Church is a "hierarchical and male-dominated culture."[42] It was not that long ago that a female bishop, Jane Dixon, was locked out of a parish church in her diocese that she tried to visit. Much of this hierarchical character is advocated by the book of polity, the *Constitution and Canons,* and even by the *Book of Common Prayer.* There are problems with the structure, not simply because men are in charge but because the nature of the hierarchical structure itself creates problems that those atop the pyramid do not seem to recognize.[43] Some male clergy feel threatened by the increasing presence of women in "their" profession because of a perceived feminization of the profession. They might even fear their own sexuality is or may be questioned if the ministry is "taken over" by women and becomes a "pink collar" profession—like nursing or teaching has been called. Whereas the situation for women in ministry has been grim, Schmidt reports that many are hopeful of brighter days ahead. Gradually people may be seeing the problem and opting for a better way.

Delores Carpenter, professor of religious education at Howard University School of Divinity, has researched the problems African American women in ministry face. In her *Profile of Black Female Master of Divinity Graduates* (book forthcoming), she reports an increase of more than 50 percent in the number of black, female Master of Divinity graduates in the United States in just four years—from 1984 to 1989 (from 300 graduates to 700)—though less than half of those are full-time pastors in a church. Yet, all the women she interviewed indicated they all finished school with the goal of ordination and hoped to be in full-time ministry. Data collected in 1992 indicates that a significant number of women have left historically African American denominations for the white, mainline churches. Carpenter reported a 16 percent loss in these African American denominations and lamented the loss to both the African American denominations and the African American community of seminary-trained leaders. The inhibitors of ministerial opportunity most often cited by these women were sexism, racism, male clergy, and the female laity who do not accept them or their ministry and have a tendency to elevate male clergy.[44]

In a 1997 lecture for "The Feminine in Religious Traditions Series" at Howard University School of Divinity, Carpenter calls these women "third wave pioneers" for their courage and for going where black women in ministry had not been allowed to go. She identifies fifteen sources of power, such as womanist theology and spirituality, that allows these women to respond meaningfully to the call of God and to utilize their educational preparation in full-time ministry. Carpenter announces the need for another Reformation to bring about renewal.

When the silent, however, find their voice, they have much to contribute, and we are all enriched. The musical group Sweet Honey and the Rock expressed this well in a song, "Sing O Barren One." Bernice Johnson Reagon composed it for the ordination of a friend. Based on Isaiah 54:1-10, the song speaks to the fact that even in one's incompleteness and woundedness and hurting, one can offer healing. In the introduction to the song Reagon writes:

> The message: To all of us who, by the standards of those who set standards—flunk—maybe we don't look right, or love right, or we don't have a home, or a job, or maybe pregnant at 14, or HIV positive, or just the wrong person, in the wrong place at the wrong time—it is You—Me, Us, who are the voices to be heard. It is We who must sing![45]

The song is about emptiness, loneliness, worthlessness, and rejection. In the context of biblical history, when a woman's highest achievement was to produce children, heirs, to be barren was to be the lowest of the low. "Sing Oh Barren One" dispels this perception of barren women as unworthy and affirms their equality and their important role in the "peopling" of the nation. The song goes:

> Empty and lonely I was
> Wordless and useless I felt
> Bounded and closed I wandered
> Empty and useless I was
>
> Then I heard The Voice
>
> Sing oh barren one
> Sing out and cry aloud
> Sing oh barren one
> Sing out and cry aloud.

Radical transformation takes place upon being able to sing. The song continues to say to the barren one that if you sing your barrenness is no more. Yahweh will make your children like nations:

> Open wide your curtains
> Enlarge the place of your tents
> Lengthen your cords
> Strengthen the stakes in the ground.
> For you will spread abroad to the right
> You will spread abroad to the left
> Your children will build nations
> I'll people your valleys
> Open wide your curtains
> Strengthen the stakes in the ground.[46]

Although women have been silenced, or their voices have not been heard in the past, Isaiah attests to the fact that they shall indeed sing. Women shall speak up in their unique voices. Deborah Tannen asserts that male-female conversation is cross-cultural communication.[47] We do believe that cross-cultural communication is possible and that understanding can take place.

Shifting Paradigms

David Thomas and Robin Ely broach an important question in an article in the *Harvard Business Review*: Why should organizations concern themselves with diversity? One answer, according to *Fortune* magazine (July 19, 1999), is that companies that pursue diversity consistently out-perform those that do not. Union Bank tops the list of the ten most diverse businesses, and their stock appreciated at a 34 percent compound annual rate for the past five years.

Occasionally the moral argument, that making a company especially friendly to diverse employees is worth doing simply because it is the right thing to do, is heard as well. Companies that launched their diversity programs did not know their efforts would necessarily pay off in financial gains—they did it because it was the right thing to do. Organizations are dealing with "customers" from all parts of the globe. It makes sense that leaders in our organizations need to be able to bridge different cultures. One executive stated, "If you are bicultural yourself, you understand that there are different ways of doing things."[48]

Thomas and Ely say that successful organizations are moving from a "discrimination-and-fairness" paradigm for dealing with diversity where everyone is treated the same to a "learning-and-effectiveness" paradigm that welcomes differences and makes the most of pluralism by incorporating all employees' perspectives into the main work of the organization in order to enhance it by rethinking primary tasks and redefining markets, products, strategies, and missions. This practice is based on the theory that race, gender, and ethnicity really do matter and that each of these identities shapes the way we do things and provides unique strengths for leadership. This paradigm differs from one that many organizations are trying to move away from—the "access-and-legitimacy" paradigm, which welcomes people of color but often tokenizes or exploits them by assigning them to work with "their own," that is African Americans handle the African American market, women handle the women's market. Instead, people of color are seen as possessing gifts for leadership in all markets and of value to the whole company. Thomas and Ely believe that "old and limiting assumptions about the meaning of diversity must be abandoned before its true potential can be realized as a powerful way to increase organizational effectiveness."[49]

Spinning Ties: Leadership for Diversity

Diversity cannot be forced. Having leaders who insist on embracing diversity may get the process started, but ultimately the will to change must come from a grassroots level. It is easier to start a new community with this vision than to change a community that does not share it. There are no easy steps to becoming a community that embraces diversity. A challenge of inclusive leadership is that change takes longer and is more difficult. It is easier for an autocratic boss to say, "We're going to do it this way."

Some of the unique characteristics of women's leadership provide a paradigm for leadership in church communities that embrace diversity and correspond to some of the characteristics of web leadership. Carol Becker describes women's leadership as process oriented, focused on the "big picture," and participatory. Women share information, have a concern for human relationships, and have the ability to negotiate. They are concerned with intimacy rather than independence and are able to do many things at once.[50] By contrast men, according to Deborah Tannen, are more concerned with freedom and independence. They are more apt to want to fix things whereas women are better able to accept ambiguity. Women do not necessarily see life as a problem to be solved; they prefer empathy and listening over problem solving. This statement is, of course, a generalization, and we realize, though women may more often use one strategy and men another, men and women may, at times, use one another's strategies.[51] Women, more than most men, are more comfortable taking the time to talk to people, connecting, and building relationships that characterize inclusive leadership. It should be noted that a study from the University of Florida found that clergywomen extend female roles of caregiving to their work as a way of overcoming resistance to their occupying a traditionally male role; this extra caring work, along with a stressful life, results in high levels of depression, and depression is one of the reasons cited for leaving the ministry. The caregiving leadership, however, is not the culprit according to many clergywomen; the culprit is the resistance to this leadership. The good news is that this style of leadership is gaining more acceptance because most people do like to be cared for. The caregiving ministry is not just a "feel-good approach," trying to make everyone happy; it is helping people connect with and care for one another.

Leadership that attempts to move toward inclusivity helps people become aware of the contradictions in the perceptions between those who are privileged and those on the fringes. Becoming conscious of the ways the fear of difference can, if we let it, lead an individual to seek to dominate another is a movement toward the commitment to change. This kind of leadership resists racism (both explicit and implicit). It discerns it and names it in order to make it possible for people to make decisions about how to act.[52]

To embrace diversity is to embrace ambiguity and change—two very threatening things, especially when the words, We've never done it that way before, have surpassed the seven last words of Christ in popularity. A preacher once said prophetically that idolatry is preferring the familiar over the infinite. It is doing the easy thing instead of the hard thing. The following story circulated on the Internet:

Primate Committee Thinking Experiment, or the Evolution of Policy

Start with a cage containing five apes. In the cage, hang a banana on a string and put stairs under it. Before long, an ape will go to the stairs and start to climb toward the banana. As soon as he touches the stairs, spray all of the apes with cold water. After a while, another ape makes an attempt with the same result—all the apes are sprayed with cold water. Turn off the cold water. If, later, another ape tries to climb the stairs, the other apes will try to prevent it even though no water sprays them. Now, remove one ape from the cage and replace it with a new one. The new ape sees the banana and wants to climb the stairs. To his horror, all of the other apes attack him. After another attempt and attack, he knows that if he tries to climb the stairs, he will be assaulted. Next, remove another of the original five apes and replace it with a new one. The newcomer goes to the stairs and is attacked. The previous newcomer takes part in the punishment with enthusiasm. Again, replace a third original ape with a new one. The new one makes it to the stairs and is attacked as well. Two of the four apes that beat him have no idea why they were not permitted to climb the stairs or why they are participating in the beating of the newest ape. After replacing the fourth and fifth original apes, all the apes that have been sprayed with cold water have been replaced. Nevertheless, no ape ever again approaches the stairs. Why not? Because that's the way it's always been around here.

Fear of change is sometimes what makes it difficult to let go of domination and subordination. It is challenging and difficult to reconceptualize the way the church works and to change the system that will carry out that work. Nevertheless, leadership is transformative, not by maintaining the status quo, but by fostering an encounter with "otherness" that transforms all who are involved. To have unity in diversity requires the renegotiation of accepted perceptions and understandings.[53]

Effective web leadership recognizes and negotiates the power dynamics between cultures and moves comfortably between cultures and diverse groups, spinning ties among them, and modeling the hospitality mandated by our tradition. It creates an environment of acceptance and aims for solidarity rather than assimilation, an environment where persons are "neither overwhelmed nor overwhelming, intimidated nor intimidating, controlled nor controlling—but interacting with the freedom of intimacy and the responsibility of mutual critique."[54] Eric Law relies on the biblical image of the wolf and lamb dwelling together to describe this phenomenon. To embrace diversity power must be shared, and people thought to be enemies or incompatible must not only coexist, but they must trust one another. Some very "unnatural" behaviors are required from all who are involved.[55] Predators and aggressors will have to refrain from devouring the weaker individuals. The weaker groups cannot run from the perceived stronger forces and will have to trust. We will have to overcome our instinct to order everything hierarchically. "We need to seek a way of relating to each other that we do not yet have or that we have long forgotten: a way of speaking about mutual relatability, intelligibility, and interdependence that goes beyond our captivity to the binary, adversarial, and oppositional discourse of human relationship."[56]

Leadership for diversity is relational and transcends special interests and ideology and moves toward common interests and goals. It develops strategies for true conversation and turn-taking. This leadership does not so much claim to be empathetic—it is obviously presumptuous for a white person to say she understands or knows how an African American woman feels. Rather, this leadership seeks to help people learn to "bracket one's own cultural assumptions"[57] and perspectives so we can "enter the other's world of assumptions, beliefs, and values and temporarily, take them as one's own."[58]

Leadership of this kind is also anticipatory.[59] It considers the business of the church to be about reforming itself as much as about reforming society. It does not wait until something happens to respond; it is proactive and, in an eschatological tone, lives in the future, moving toward that vision of God. "We should not pursue racial or cultural diversity simply because it is politically correct (or incorrect, as the case may be), or because it is the latest theological fad, or even because it is a good conservative or liberal idea. We should do it because it is the gospel."[60]

To understand, respect, embrace, and accept diversity in the church is not enough. Diversity must move us to action, specifically to a commitment to social justice. We already have a diversity of cultures in our churches, though many are still segregated in practice and some will continue to feel threatened with a loss of identity. Perhaps our challenge is to decide, now, how to help people in the church deal with their deepest differences. It is time for partnerships, coalition building, covenant communities (more on this in chapter 5), and clusters of churches working together on social justice agendas, shared staffing, networking, and web leadership based on our mission and Christian traditions.

In Spanish this forward motion is called *Adelante!* and we heartily call for it. Diversity is a promise for the church, a confrontation with otherness that invites us to transformation. As Delores Carpenter has said, this is truly "a kairos moment"[61] for the church in which the time of significant change is near. It might not happen tomorrow or the next day or even the day after that, but hold on and keep the faith, for change is a comin'! In the selecting and refining of the metaphor of the web for leadership, one key, we believe, is education—both in the sense that the leader teaches and transforms to embrace diversity and in the sense that there is education for this kind of leadership. As we teach for discipleship, we must change how we do it in our multicultural, cross-cultural, and transnational ministries. In the next chapter we explore pedagogical foundations for teaching for diversity. Any change or shift or movement has to do the hard work of education and of communicating its message.

New Rules for the Church

- Pray often.
- Seek common ground for the playing field.
- Choose no sides; everybody plays together.
- Invite the spectators into the game.
- Whoever has the ball, leads.
- Pass the ball often to get the maximum benefit.
- Cooperate rather than compete, and everybody wins.
- Honor differences as sacred and valuable.
- Choose to reward effort rather than results.
- Go "out of bounds" when necessary for Jesus.
- Pray always.

CHAPTER FOUR

The Web and Pedagogy

We know that changing what *we teach means changing* how *we teach.*
MARGO CULLY ET AL., GENDERED SUBJECTS

The shape of our knowledge becomes the shape of our living.
PARKER PALMER, TO KNOW AS WE ARE KNOWN

I am a teacher at heart, and there are moments in the classroom when I can hardly hold the joy.
PARKER PALMER, THE COURAGE TO TEACH

Wherein lies the hope for those of us worn down by the hierarchical and patriarchal leadership in the church and by the resistance to diversity? We believe that education is a key to change in the current system. This change, we believe, may happen in three ways: in modeling web-like leadership in teaching, which influences the church and society, in preparing a new generation of leaders for the church, and in preparing the church for this new kind of leadership.

Like many of the social justice educators of this century, we believe that education can be an effective means for change and a way to challenge oppressive systems that inhibit web leadership. If the goal is "full and equal participation of all groups in society and in the church," as stated in the last chapter, then this chapter seeks to outline a process, a pedagogy, for implementing this goal in the church. To achieve this goal the process has to model the goal. It should be inclusive, participatory, experiential, and affirming.[1] There might be particular learning opportunities to deal specifically with diversity, but the pedagogy presented here is meant to facilitate the embracing of diversity and the sharing of leadership in *all* learning opportunities.

It is not an accident that we focus on education as the key to change or on the "how" of education since we are both Christian educators. Homiletics, or preaching, can also be a force of change; however, it offers limited possibilities for several reasons. One is that preaching today tends to be geared toward making people feel good, to giving them comfort, a "warm fuzzy feeling," and to promoting a "Jesus and Me" relationship. This highlights personal growth rather than change in the church or society. Another reason is that preaching can be misused as an avenue for the preacher to look good, to "shine." The focus is on the preacher rather than the word. Entertainment value becomes the measuring stick for what constitutes good preaching. Rick Warren, Pastor of Saddleback Community Church, once asked a group of preachers, "Are you trying to impress your seminary professor or God when you preach?"[2] The key word here is *impress*. Should preaching be to impress? We do not think God is easily impressed. Perhaps we can aim to please God through our teaching and preaching, but the emphasis on trying to look good so that God will like us is just one more kind of works righteousness.[3] Even when preaching is prophetic and speaks eloquently in the name of social justice, the communication is often "one-way." There is little opportunity or potential for the hearer to interact with and dialogue about the concepts and ideas voiced. This preaching may inspire one to love God and seek justice, but at some point, a person has to think about it—to reflect on the God he or she serves through a process of education and formation. Education is the means by which people both teach and practice what they preach.

One kind of preaching that can capture the spirit of web of leadership comes from the African American tradition. Evans Crawford and Thomas Troeger, in *The Hum: Call and Response in African American Preaching*, describe preaching as a folk art that promotes a call and response. It is an oral event or "participant proclamation." The church attempts to foster resonance through its liturgy. The congregation listens for something they relate to and when they hear it, sounds it back to the preacher, an "effective expression of the priesthood of the entire group."[4] If we want to speak to the postmodern sight-and-sound generation, we have to find such methods to replace the "sit-and-soak worship,"[5] using Leonard Sweet's terminology.

There is a close relationship between teaching and preaching. One is not "above" the other in ministry, nor is education without its limitations. Both preaching and teaching are the ministry of the Word; the content is the same. James Smart, Bible scholar and educator from several decades ago, helped bridge the schism between teaching and preaching in *The Teaching Ministry of the Church*. He pointed out the critical nature of teaching in the church, something that was often sublated by other forms of ministry.[6] Preaching is often viewed as coming from the sacred realm while teaching is "from below," just some of our ordinary human groanings. While this may not be an accurate theological description, it has been, and may still be, common thinking. It is precisely at this place of ordinary human groaning that educators do their most extraordinary, sacred work, not through didactic means normally associated with teaching—of lecturing and "filling heads"—but through the relational and experiential means of listening to and understanding our groanings. Ronnie Prevost wrote about the "Prophetic Voice of the Religious Educator," claiming that cultural differences and conflict are of particular concern for religious education as teachers can emphasize *koinonia* as content and use the methodology of genuine dialogue.[7]

Conventional Education

We acknowledge that education has its limitations. Even as we examine pedagogical traditions and epistemologies (ways of knowing) for just leadership or even web leadership, we are cognizant of traditional or conventional educational practices that have worked against social justice. Academia is usually notoriously hierarchical and competitive, the same condition that we have been critiquing in the church. Many students have carried that habit of competition into all aspects of their life and relationships. Most of us were steeped in the "lecture and discussion" mode of traditional education that promotes dualistic thinking. This form of education seeks clear answers, unambiguous data, and external authority. Conventional education's function is to produce an idealized vision of society in which everyone knows his or her place.[8] Parker Palmer critiques "a way of knowing that treats the world as an object to be dissected and manipulated, a way of knowing that gives us power over the world."[9] This sort of knowing is bent on winning, getting ahead, and getting the A. Opportunistic and arrogant, it is a way of knowing that brings violence to the world by its frontierism—the quest to be first, to be the best. It is a "kind of knowing that begins and ends in human pride and power."[10]

The motivation for this type of knowledge is control and dominance and the desire to manipulate the world to our own ends. Knowledge for control and power creates distances between people. Traditional modes of teaching for this kind of knowledge may create barriers that prevent us from getting to the "meat" of the issues. Palmer calls this "Objectivism." Objectivism assumes a sharp distinction between the knower and the known. Objects passively exist, waiting for us to conquer them. In Martin Buber's terms, objectivism fosters an I-It rather than an I-Thou relationship. Teaching for objectivism depends on the imitation of authority, not on original thinking, and assumes the human mind is a "blank slate."[11] There has been and still is an academic bias against subjectivity. Academic culture encourages a disconnected life. Academics have a tendency to write in the passive voice because that is what we were taught and because it helps us to keep our distance, to keep from getting all tangled up in our subject, from getting "messy." Many postmodern scientists and philosophers now question that objectivity; they say that "neutral" facts are never truly neutral.

The Christian belief in the Incarnation says that Jesus got all tangled up with us. Truth is personal and communal, not propositional. Jesus, as the way, the truth, and the life, came and lived among us. Yes, it got messy. Messiness is inherent in the Incarnation. Latinos, according to theologian Hal Recinos, have a strong sense that Jesus "pitches God's tent among the poor" then relate "his message to the world of overlooked people."[12] Still this whitewashed, sterilized, and sanitized epistemology and pedagogy persists, even in the church. Teachers cling to conventional pedagogy because it gives them power and prestige. Students cling to it because of a fear of the unknown and because it gives them security. It is easier to be told exactly what to do to get the A. Students that are "held hostage" in the classroom to fulfill some kind of requirement may even resent being asked to interact or discuss. One student told a teacher who was trying to model a more relational style that she did not feel she was getting her money's worth out of the class if she did not leave with a composition notebook full of notes.

To learn is always to change. Conventional education avoids a knowledge that calls for our conversion.[13] Students fear making a mistake, looking bad, or saying the wrong thing. They are afraid of being challenged, of not getting credit, and of conflicting with others. Silence in the classroom is often the defense. Women in particular feel this defensiveness that leads to silence; Maria Harris calls silence the "first and resounding experience in women's education."[14] Fear discourages us from experimenting with truth, which allows us to weave a wider web of connectedness.[15] To eliminate fear in both the teacher and the students, conventional pedagogies simplify the world by reducing it to an object to be examined, analyzed, mastered, and ultimately owned rather than portraying it as "a community of selves and spirits related to each other in a complex web of accountability called 'truth.' "[16]

We have named some of the marginalized groups in society and in the church. Have we considered that students are among the most marginalized in our society? With traditional pedagogies of dominance and submission, we have prompted and played to their fears and sent students to the edge, sometimes literally. We have done this in may ways: by not recognizing their experience, their culture, their perspective, and their personhood and making them park the farthest distance from the center of our campuses—both metaphorically and geographically! We have created impossible and silly hoops for them to jump through in the name of "paying one's dues." Subconsciously or consciously, if they are honest, teachers see themselves as far above their students in knowledge and ability. We have insisted that our way of knowing is best and that they must know in the same way we do.

Research done by Mary Belenky and others in *Women's Ways of Knowing* found that listening is one way of knowing, and for women it is a listening both to learn from others and to learn from the self by listening to the inner voice. Women, much less than men, do see the need to align themselves with a particular authority, yet conventional education is geared toward a male preference for an external authority. That subjective or intuitive knowing is very important in web leadership where authority is not external—not something imposed upon us but something that comes from the inside out. This does not mean that anyone can be a self-proclaimed authority. For true inner authority to emerge, years of experience and learning have to happen. Belenky called this epistemological orientation "connected knowing" as opposed to "separate knowing," which is knowledge based on following a set of agreed upon rules. Separate knowing can be defensive and adversarial. Women seek access and connection to other people's knowledge.[17] Some of these researchers' findings, though from more than a decade ago, help us to appropriate an understanding of the role of education in extending web leadership.

Education for a Web Way of Knowing

There is another kind of knowledge that springs from compassion and has the goal of unity and of healing our brokenness. It is a desire to "recreate the organic community in which the world was first created."[18] It is a *yada* kind of knowledge from the Hebrew scriptures meaning "to be intimate with," as in "Abraham knew Sarah." If knowledge for control and power creates distances between people, knowledge based on love creates connective tissue between people. It is a way of knowing that overcomes separation and alienation and draws people into relationships, into a community of mutual learning, face-to-face, but a knowledge that springs from love will implicate us in the web of life; it will wrap the knower and the known in compassion, which is a bond of awesome responsibility as well as transforming joy. It will call us to involvement, mutuality, and accountability.[19]

We both are very familiar with and have long been graced by the works of Parker Palmer. We had not noticed until now, however, how much he relies on the metaphor of the web in developing his pedagogy. He refers to the web, the connective tissue of life: "Reality is a web of communal relationships, and we can know reality only by being in community with it."[20] Mary Elizabeth Moore wrote that organic metaphors that describe human beings in a web or relationship are promising for education as an alternative to mechanistic, outcome-oriented education.[21] This way of knowing engenders specific ways to teach, so we describe what we think a web pedagogy would look like in the movement toward just leadership.

A Web Pedagogy

Our description of a web pedagogy is similar to the description of social justice or critical education, or conscientizing as it is sometimes called, and these conscience-raising pedagogies have been crucial for marginalized peoples. There are some specific characteristics and methods, from which pedagogy could call forth a web-like leadership in the church, which we will name. A web pedagogy creates a space, an ethos, where there is openness, boundaries, and hospitality. Architecture alone will not do it. A church in the round may appear to signify a collaborative community but may only be a facade for a staged setting for the ascension of a "star." In a web-modeled environment there is space and freedom to explore, yet there are boundaries and ground rules of mutual respect that are observed. A web pedagogy offers hospitality and invites people into the weaving and reweaving of the social fabric.

A web pedagogy might be best understood by outlining one process for its development. We adapted these steps from *Teaching for Diversity and Social Justice* by Adams, Bell, and Griffin.

1) Pre-assessment and goal setting. This involves finding out as much as possible about students before the learning opportunity begins. Who is to be taught is as important as what is to be taught. Is this a homogeneous group? What might they have in common? How might they differ? It also means providing structure or boundaries by naming expectations and goals for the course.

2) Creating an environment. We recently mentioned hospitality. It is important that each student is validated and not made to feel invisible. If the climate is perceived as threatening, students will feel inhibited or thwarted in the process of self-disclosure. This pedagogy attends to the experiences and needs of the student and accommodates a variety of learning styles and preferences without stereotyping the individual through uncritical application of learning styles or the multiple intelligence theory. A web pedagogy balances the emotional and cognitive aspects of learning. In the conventional classroom there is little or no place for emotion—a display of feeling is perceived as awkward or embarrassing—but this pedagogy recognizes that learning is not just a matter of appropriating a set of facts but also a means of grappling with feelings and assumptions. There is a need to create a safe place where people are comfortable sharing their emotions, especially ones that are perceived as negative, such as anger, fear, or pain.[22] The teacher's authority is used as a bridge to overcome the traditional teacher-student hierarchy. Conventional top-down teaching does not prepare students for the complexities of the world. This pedagogy challenges the traditional class-room hierarchy in order to build a community of learn-ing. Teaching here is mediation, maieutic or midwifery, and drawing out and bringing forth voices—what Nelle Morton called "hear[ing] people to speech."[23]

One technique that might be used is the classic Socratic method, developed around the fifth century and described in the *Apologia*. This method involves holding conversation. It is asking questions that elicit "ideas [people] had not even realized." It is skillful questioning that gently guides someone from unexam-ined assumptions to a more reflective consideration. It engages the learner in responsible thought and the obtainment of the truth by means of questioning. It can be a way of dismantling arrogance without the use of arrogance by the educator. The method has been called penetrating and probing and even "annoying" by our students when we've used it. They have also grinned with glee in some cases. Sally Helgesen sees it as con-ducive to web leadership.[24] Socrates made himself available and frequented the *agora*, or marketplace; from this central position, his role actually became more characteristic of the periphery. By his actions he joined the center and the margin, "building tendrils of connection that established a true web of inclusion."[25] Maria Harris wrote that learning "consists of posing questions that lead us to realize that in our own per-sons, we are the essential questions that life presents. . . . The posing of questions is at the heart of connected knowing."[26]

3) Recognizing and examining our own cultural embedment. The web pedagogy begins with people's real-life experience and helps us to understand how our social identities shape our thinking. According to Belenky, the most trustworthy knowledge comes from personal experience.[27] This is a pedagogy that is helpful to marginalized people because it is characterized by an emphasis on everyday life—not something "out there" and foreign to them.[28] This emphasis on experience is not relativism; it is not saying that one way of looking at reality is as good as another or that my experience determines reality for me, and your experience determines reality for you. The "anything goes" perspective results in a weak understanding of diversity, as we have said previously. The uncritical and unexamined acceptance of all points of view does not connect the dots and "concedes diversity without calling us into dialogue."[29] Web pedagogy is a pedagogy that utilizes experience and critical reflection. Students are active coinvestigators. This learning opportunity might begin with low-risk self-disclosure—introductions, storytelling—and move toward riskier disclosure. In this pedagogy teachers may challenge and condemn stereotypes and prejudice, but ultimately it is the student who must decide to rid himself or herself of those ideas.

4) Confronting differences. When sharing perspectives, there will be differences. Instead of trying to have everybody agree and have a discussion that doesn't go anywhere, invite divergent perspectives and allow tensions and contradictions to emerge. Web pedagogy affirms individuals while facilitating group interaction at the same time, and it is attentive to the social relationships in the classroom. A technique known as processing may take place here. Processing is an intentional and systematically guided discussion that encourages the expression of divergent perspectives and allows for both cognitive and experiential learning. It requires monitoring and involves individual reflection, descriptions of reactions, talk about thoughts and feelings, and analysis of issues, questions, and concerns. It then moves to summary or closure and understanding where there was agreement or disagreement. Afterward there is application: how might the new learning be applied. This is exploring new territory, and the terrain can be rough. But the learning we will gain is worth the bruises along the way.

5) Allowing the disequilibrium to work. In confronting differences there may be some discomfort when one is on her or his learning edge, when one's values, beliefs, and assumptions are challenged. There can be confusion and resistance. The teacher does not try to provide answers. "Culturally relevant teachers maintain equitable and reciprocal teacher-student relations within which student expertise is highlighted, teachers encourage their entire classes rather than singling out single learners, and students are partly responsible for each others' academic success." The web pedagogy allows the process to work. "Culturally relevant teachers see knowledge as doing, discuss their pedagogical choices and strategies with their students, and teach actively against a 'right-answer approach.' "[30]

6) Integrating. This is the new foundation that is built, the new footing that the learning brings. Upon integrating the new learning there is change in the individual and in the community. The teacher helps students see themselves as agents of change.

The sequencing or progression in this pedagogy might use a "see, judge, act" progression or one identified by

David Kolb in his experiential learning model, which accommodates for a variety of learning styles. This progression moves from concrete experience (touching, hearing, seeing, observing) to reflective observation (silence, journals, discussion, brainstorming) to abstract conceptualization (lecturing, reading, writing) to active experimentation (action projects, doing).[31]

Another meaningful basis for teaching and leading in the Christian community that has been around for some time and has been articulated by Thomas Groome is the "shared praxis" approach. Groome describes it as "a group of Christians sharing in dialogue their critical reflection on present action in light of the Christian Story and its Vision toward the end of lived Christian faith."[32] This sequencing involves naming present action, experience, and the way we express who we are; critically reflecting on that experience to evaluate the present; looking at what the scripture and tradition says about the topic utilizing "creative memory to uncover the past in the present"; dialectically moving between experience and tradition (that is, what does the community's story mean for our story, and how do our stories respond to the community's story); and choosing a personal faith response.[33]

Despite the fact that social justice pedagogies have been articulated by various people from a variety of settings since the 1960s, they still are not the norm in practice. One reason for the slow pace of change, as we have pointed out, is that this kind of teaching is not always the easy way. Therefore many teachers give up on it. Or, as some social scientists have noted, just because ideas change, doesn't mean our practice will, but Parker Palmer believes that practice will follow. He says, "the transformation of teaching must begin in the transformed heart of the teacher."[34]

The Web Teacher

In a web pedagogy the identity and integrity of the teacher are of ultimate importance. "Good teachers possess a capacity for connectedness. They are able to weave a complex web of connection among themselves, their subjects, and their students so that students can learn to weave a world for themselves."[35]

One woman who answered a clear calling to teaching in higher education described to us her personal diminishment. She learned that in order to fulfill her vocation she would have to "make herself" over to conform to academic standards of excellence. That meant a new, "acceptable" vocabulary and an unnatural projection of herself sitting upon some pedestal at a "high level" that made her feel ridiculous and unconnected. She learned how to "talk," but she equated it to an immigrant being forced to speak English as a child. The academic language that she learned was a language she admired, yet she felt diminished while speaking it. Eventually she could no longer keep up the facade. Fortunately, she had "made it enough" in the academic world that she had the luxury of rejecting it in order to be true to herself. She was able to restore her sense of identity and her integrity as a person and as a teacher.

Too often, people confuse identity with technique—being with doing. The two are integrally bound up with each other, but there is a distinction. According to Palmer, technique is what teachers use until the real teacher shows up. There are techniques (and we have named some of them previously) that usually reveal, rather than close up, personhood. Most techniques, however, can be turned around and used negatively.

More important than technique is the art of teaching, the organic process that encourages relationships.[36] *Modeling web leadership in teaching teaches web leadership.*

114

Web teachers work out from the center of their class-rooms, whether the settings are formal or informal; they are always reaching outward to include others in the decision making and deriving their "power" and "authority" from their accessibility. This accessibility allows the teacher to form and shape her or his students and not just fill their "empty" heads with information they may very well forget. Increased access to information in virtually all facets of life is growing so fast that traditional ways of teaching are being challenged by students who do not think they even need personal access to "live" teachers because they have the Internet! While the computer cannot replace the person, we still must think of new ways to teach and to bring our gifts and ourselves to our students in such a way that they will listen and respond.

Teaching is a sacred thing, a very personal, yet communal, thing. In the church, teaching is particularly an expression of the sacred model of "walking with," dwelling with, and being surprised by the presence of the teacher, the rabbi—Jesus, in the case of Christians. The biblical story of the walk to Emmaus, found in Luke 24, is illustrative of this. Often this story is used to convey the difference a personal relationship with Jesus Christ can make in one's life. Indeed, the Walk to Emmaus, an admirable and veritable movement in the United Methodist Church with counterparts in other denominations, uses the "walk" as a metaphor for the renewal of one's faith.

The passage in Luke 24 also illustrates web leadership and teaching. Consider some of the details of the story. After Jesus' crucifixion and death, a couple of his followers were walking to Emmaus from Jerusalem. They were somewhat aimless, depressed, confused, and discouraged about the events they had seen. (Is this the state of the church today?) A stranger appears and falls in step with them. He inquires about their consternation, which

115

shows on their faces. The disciples confide their disillusionment. They start the story of their woes. Had they
been had? Had they been misled? They express their sad-
ness and disorientation as they tell the story of the crucifixion of their Lord. The "stranger" has listened intently
to their story. He then asks them a question. (Socratic
method!) It is a question that invites them to consider
what they actually believe. It is a question that is gently
corrective, a loving admonition. Had they forgotten their
passion from before? What happened to their enthusiasm, their new understanding? The stranger then pro-
ceeds to *crack open the book*, to read the text in a new way
that speaks to their woes. He interprets the scriptures,
bringing a new "hearing" to them in light of their recent
experience of their leader's death. Upon enlightenment,
the stranger breaks bread with them in the tradition of
hospitality of the times. Upon *cracking open the bread*,
there is a new learning, a new enlightenment, a hospitality that both nourishes and reveals. The disciples suddenly recognize Jesus, the stranger, as their risen Lord.

When we teach, giving encouragement takes effort
and discipline, but it is rewarding to participate in an
environment of mutual support. When we do this, we
heed that essential counsel to "outdo one another in
showing honor" (Rom. 12:10), and we pattern our teaching after Jesus. Jesus was a ceaselessly encouraging
teacher whose followers became a sign of his up-build-
ing presence in the world.[37] The Scriptures have more
words for how this learning relationship works between
student and teacher: "Let the word of Christ dwell in
you richly; teach and admonish one another in all wisdom; and with gratitude in you hearts sing psalms,
hymns, and spiritual songs to God" (Col. 3:16).

The characteristics of weblike teaching are becoming
obvious; here is a list of some of them. The web teacher
or leader:

- walks with and spends time with his or her students
- listens to the students' experiences
- is present among the students and builds trust
- validates the students' experiences
- questions the students
- challenges the students' understandings
- cracks open the book to look for new insights
- interprets and helps the disciples interpret for themselves
- cracks open the bread—opens up and reveals himself or herself in a sacramental way

Though technique, we have said, is not the way to implement a web pedagogy, the Emmaus narrative demonstrates some of the techniques that are effective. One way to encourage relationship is through narrative, doing what the stranger did in retelling the story of the tradition. This can involve many techniques that tap the imagination, such as storytelling, drama, film, and role playing, which is particularly effective for a listening way of knowing and for spinning relational ties. In any case, the focus of the teacher is on the subject—not in accumulating information about it, but rather in being attentive to it—and her students, encouraging students to use their knowledge in the world. Teachers can create a hospitable space where "we know ourselves not as isolated atoms threatened by otherness but as integral parts of the great web of life."[38] Anthropologist and educator Mary Catherine Bateson reflecting on her own teaching and the connections she tries to make in *Peripheral Visions: Learning Along the Way*, says:

> A professor is supposed to be authoritative and well prepared, so it is hard to resist offering answers without questions and conveying the message that the world is

divided between those who know and those who do not. My own greatest resource as a teacher is the learned willingness to wing it in public, knowing that I will be faced with unexpected questions, some of which I cannot answer. This is the challenge—improvising, learning on the job—that my students will confront all their lives. Oddly, I find myself trying to convey two contrasting ideas. On the one hand, I try to teach students to benefit from difference instead of being put off by it. On the other hand, I find myself discouraging the notion that learning depends on that specific difference we call authority.[39]

The Web Learner

As we teach and lead in postmodern society we need to understand how postmodern people think and learn. Leonard Sweet claims the current young generations are transitional to a new age. The new millennium, globalization, and cybernetics are changing the world. A recent newspaper advertisement expressed this change numerically: 1,729 languages, 196 cultures, 143 religions—all converging in cyberspace. A German scholar, Frederic Vester, did work on the theory of cybernetics back in 1980. Cybernetics is radically different from Aristotelian logic that connects cause and effect in straight lines. Cybernetic thinking operates in circular motions, or "closed control loops," where causes become effects and effects causes and where a person can enter the loop from any entry point. Reasoning is not done in a "logical, linear fashion but through a series of links and a multitude of connections, juxtapositions, and adjacencies."[40] Cybernetics is the instrument for this new age, where everything happens with electronic velocity. Distances and spaces are being altered. Cybernetic speed has altered the meaning of the verb "to be." Virtuality is a new space where we are able to conjugate "to be" in a distinct manner without physical presence or direct contact being necessary. Technology allows us to be in two places at the same time. According to Leonard Sweet, "Postmoderns can't draw a straight line."[41] If the culture is thinking in "control loops," what does that mean for teaching and leading?

Mary Catherine Bateson describes learning as a double helix, a spiraling in which going over the same ground represents layers of change and increasing understanding. Most learning, she writes, "is not linear."[42] Yet in planning for teaching, we often present material in linear sequences—one concept must be grasped before another is presented. This method can make the classroom threatening to some. Learning outside the classroom is not like that at all. Something that is too complex to grasp the first time spirals past again and again revealing more and more to the learner. Bateson's book *Peripheral Visions* equates learning with our untapped circular vision. We do not just see what is straight ahead, what is out in front of us, but we see and learn what is out on the edges—all around us—in order to get fuller understanding.

Learning, understood as circular and relational, is not new. The work of Janice Hale-Benson on the learning styles of black children notes that ethnicity emerged as a primary factor in distinct patterns of mental ability. Using Rosalie Cohen's identification of two learning styles, analytical and relational, Hale-Benson talks about the relational abilities of black children and their attempts to function in schools that are geared for analytical thinking. Pupils who have a different cognitive style will not only be poor achievers early in school, but they will also have more learning difficulties as they move to higher grade levels.[43] Now, however, researchers have discovered that ethnic children may not be the only ones who learn this way. The overall decline of school performance supports this finding.

The web learner comes to every learning opportunity open and ready to learn, and the learning field of the classroom is level. Every student from whatever perspective, culture, gender, or class has equal access to learning. Barbara Omolade writes about a feminist pedagogy that empowers students, helping them to make sense of what they already know. The creation of the intellectual partnership lessens the power imbalance yet reinforces the knowledge that can be received and shared from the instructor, from the readings, and from each other.[44] The responsibility for learning is shared by the student, the teacher, and the other learners—the community of the classroom. The web learner does not expect to be handed the "answers" or told how to do things outside the classroom. This pedagogy is not about learning a bag of tricks. Students listen, think, converse, and question. Radically, they may not take notes. They might write down some reflections or jot down some ideas to pursue at a later time, but it is pointless to write down everything a teacher says as if taking dictation. There are tape recorders for that. Web teachers will often provide an outline of important concepts. Taking notes is more distracting than helpful because the student is concentrating on writing down the words and not thinking or interacting with the material. It is the interaction that moves the class forward to the next learning goal.

The web learner knows that learning is not limited to the classroom and formal opportunities. This kind of learner asks questions everywhere she goes, scans every book he sees, hones in on every opportunity he can to challenge, refine, select, rethink, and evaluate.

The Story of Ada

A woman came mysteriously into our congregation recently. Her name was Ada, and she let us know in a hurry that she had never been to church before and was just "exploring." After she had explored for a year or so, her gifts for ministry emerged quite remarkably. She began with "bite-sized" forms of ministry—small, but not insignificant tasks. Because of her conscientiousness, she was invited into a larger leadership position. Yet, unschooled in the ways and means of church life, she immediately began bumping up against policies, procedures, precedents, and the often repeated phrase, "But we've never done it like that before," while trying to do her ministry. She was from a culture that was different from most in this particular congregation, and to some, her accent made her difficult to understand. As bumpy as her journey was, Ada was a breath of fresh air. She was constantly bombarding the church staff with questions. She signed up for training classes, continuing education, any event related to Christian ministry that was available to laypeople and that she could afford.

No one knew it at the time she joined us, but Ada eventually revealed that she was a survivor. She had fled to the United States from El Salvador in the 1980s and changed her name out of fear for her life, and she had survived cancer. Ada was used to getting to the truth of things and would not settle for less. She had had to ask her doctors the difficult questions about her cancer, so she simply continued that methodology and asked the hard questions of her church. She questioned our worship and our educational ministries. She questioned the lackluster way we did business, even the ethics of it! She bore an uncanny resemblance to the lad in the story of "The Emperor's New Clothes." She called the congregation's attention to some things we did every year without question, without regard to purpose or worthwhileness. And she wanted to do some things that were unconventional for this particular congregation. She wanted to throw a block party to celebrate Pentecost. She wanted to host a monthly birthday party for children in the community who were not necessarily part of the church. She wanted to write a letter to the bishop protesting a decision the church had made. A few supportive people persisted with her ideas though there were some "buts." ("But it might mess up the church lawn." "But why can't the community center do that?" "But who is going to plan that and take care of the details?" "But we might get in trouble with the conference, and besides that's not your job.")

Sometimes Ada became frustrated. We were afraid she'd give up and leave. Some of us were constantly trying to mend fences. One day she simply said, "You don't need to defend me. I'm here." We had forgotten that she was a survivor. "I'm here," she said. This meant a million things. It meant: "I'm in here; I'm not absent; I can defend myself." It also meant: "I'm here; I'm among you, you don't have to worry. Things will work out; I'm not going to leave." It meant: "I am a leader; I will accept the sacred responsibility with which I've been charged." It was a comforting thing to hear Ada say, "I'm here."

Ada challenged the way we did things. The sheer freshness of it awed us, bowled the church over. Ada was asked to be a teacher—not that she had not been a teacher before—but she was given a formal forum. In the classroom she continued to ask her difficult questions; she made it clear that she was there to learn as much as the members of her class. Her class attracted throngs of people (at least for that congregation where ten to twenty people constituted a throng). These were people who just liked talking with Ada. Her students said, "She knows how to ask questions; she knows how to listen; she knows how to help us say what we are feeling and thinking." If there was a controversial topic or question hiding in any corner of any conversation, Ada would find it. Ada would ask us why we did certain things the way we did and make us confront the fact that we did not know why we did some of these things, and we came face-to-face with the fact that we probably should not do them. She had her detractors, but she, more than anyone or anything else, shook that congregation out of its slumberous, maintenance mode. It wasn't just that the conflict stirred us, we had had conflict before. It was her relentless relationality that let people know they could not ignore her, that she was a force to be reckoned with. She was political without being political—meaning she aimed for change, but she did not do it in the traditional way of "divide and conquer." She did it by trial and error, much like she fought her cancer—trying new things, new approaches, always questioning, seeking, and networking. Yet it never occurred to her to do anything else. This was just something natural for her to do, with no hidden agendas, no axes to grind, no ladders to climb. It suddenly struck some of us that we were blessed to be in the presence of a beautiful and rare gem of a creature with many facets—an authentic leader, web maker, teacher, and woman (to name a few).

Teaching Teachers to Teach Using a Web Pedagogy

A surprised look comes across the faces of students taking the course on church Bible study at Howard University School of Divinity when they learn that the course will be noncompetitive, and that they will share in the leadership. After all, why should the teacher be the only one that learns to teach? The course begins with the reading of the Beatitudes from *The Message* by Eugene Peterson. Theologians have said that the Sermon on the Mount is a prescription for a spiritually healthy and whole life. This passage sets the tone for the teaching and learning environment of the course. Jesus' message is paraphrased to say:

"You're blessed when you're content with just who you are—no more, no less. That's the moment you find yourselves proud owners of everything that can't be bought. . . . You're blessed when you care. At the moment of being 'care-full,' you find yourselves cared for. . . . You're blessed when you can show people how to cooperate instead of compete or fight. That's when you discover who you really are and your place in God's family. . . . Not only that—count yourselves blessed every time people put you down or throw you out or speak lies about you to discredit me. What it means is that the truth is too close for comfort, and they are uncomfortable. You can be glad when that happens— give a cheer even!—for though they don't like it, *I* do! And all heaven applauds. And know that you are in good company. My prophets and witnesses have always gotten into this kind of trouble." *(The Message)*

Students learn that they can be themselves, that they are valued for who they are, and they learn that they do not have to perform or play it safe. The learning experience in the classroom is a modeling of this biblical prescription that they can take with them. By the time the course has ended and the students have had an opportunity to teach themselves, they realize they have experienced a new teaching methodology, a web pedagogy.

To encourage students to write their own church Bible study based on types rather than being limited to topics or book-by-book or traditional lectionary Bible study, students are given a sampling of different types of Bible study and a bibliography that identifies resources for teaching each type. Students are invited to use their imaginations and find ways to "bring the message home"—to make it relevant in today's world to diverse groups of people.

Together, both in and outside of class, the students engage in exegetical work using *Biblical Interpretation: A Roadmap* by Frederick Tiffany and Sharon Ringe, *Stony the Road We Trod* by Cain Hope Felder, and *Church Bible Study*

Handbook by Robin Maas. In order to build skills with tools of biblical interpretation, the students and the teacher work together in the library for a "hands-on" experience. Students build a common vocabulary and work in teams searching for scriptures that are appropriate for the types of Bible study that are suggested. Students give in-class teaching demonstrations of a variety of types of Bible study that they design and write based on guided preparations from the teacher. Time is spent in class going over the exegetical work, discussing the reading assignments, observing the demonstrations of both the teacher and other students, and moving from interpretation to action to product. A joint list consisting of scriptures and possible or appropriate types of Bible study for that scripture as a guide for teaching and leading Bible study in the students' respective church settings is developed. Students discuss how they would lead Bible study in various contexts, such as the following:

- regarding disabled persons—2 Samuel 4:4
- regarding prostitutes—Matthew 11:19
- regarding persons who are HIV positive or have AIDS—Luke 17
- regarding abused women—Isaiah 54:1-8; Matthew 18:1-6
- regarding age, culture, or gender specific groups—Acts 8:26-40
- regarding homeless people—Mark 7:24-30; Luke 16:19-31
- regarding prisoners—Psalm 146; Philippians 1; Matthew 26:47-68

This community-building exercise illustrates weblike teaching that includes and informs every student in the class. There is no hierarchical position among the students because of their abilities, and the teacher is not a ruling authoritarian but a co-learner, more often than not sitting in a "learning circle" with the students. People are motivated not by being pitted against one another but by being a community. The distinctive and intertwining web leadership is inclusive, and there is no place for exclusivity as the Word of God is taken into the new century.

The Church and Diversity

The following course design is for adults in a local congregation (it could be adapted for persons from several different congregations) for the purpose of exploring diversity, enhancing a congregation's positive response to diversity, and helping congregations deal with challenges that arise in a diverse community. This course is only one part of a more thorough, ongoing process of embracing diversity. We are indebted to the work of Adams, Bell, and Griffin in *Teaching for Diversity and Social Justice: A Sourcebook* and to Cathy Tamsberg, who was the student intern at Calvary Baptist Church in Washington, D.C. at the time. It may be useful (but not necessary) to create a software presentation when teaching this course. The course is designed for twelve to fifteen participants, ideally. We suggest a retreat format, although the three, three- hour sessions may be divided into shorter segments. The facilitator should be a person well versed in leading fruitful discussions and someone who will be an active participant, encourage disclosure, and be able to guide learning should anger or other emotions be expressed.

A Curriculum Design

Learning Goals

- To create dialogue on diversity and to build community.
- To raise awareness of oppressive assumptions,

beliefs, and institutional manifestations of racism and sexism.

- To gain conceptual understanding of "isms" and their consequences.
- To explore biblical understandings of diversity and leadership.
- To help congregations explore steps they can take toward embracing diversity.

Materials Needed

- Newsprint
- Markers
- Tape
- Bibles (different translations), Bible commentaries, Bible dictionaries, other help guides
- Pencils
- Songbooks, hymnals
- Index cards
- Multicolored yarn

Session 1: Barriers to Diversity (Time needed: approximately 3 hours)

I. Welcome and introductions

As participants arrive give them a name tag and an index card. Ask them to write an expectation they have for the course on one side of the card. On the other side, have them write down a fear or concern they have about the course. They should not write their names on the cards. When everyone has arrived and completed their cards, collect the cards, mix them up, and redistribute them. Participants then introduce themselves by telling something about themselves then reading aloud the expectation and fear on the card they received. Leaders should also introduce themselves in the same way. Tell the class that the session will encourage a safe environment where these concerns are addressed. Offer prayer for the hopes and fears of the course.

II. Review learning goals and housekeeping details
Go over the goals and any details. Agree on guidelines for discussion, which may include:

- Confidentiality
- Openness to opposing viewpoints
- Respectful disagreement
- Self-monitoring of speaking up (each person will agree to allow everyone who wishes an opportunity to speak to have his or her chance, before speaking a second or third time)

III. Bible study
The story of Pentecost. Make sure each participant has a Bible. Ask them to find Acts 2. Ask for volunteers to read a portion of the scripture until the entire chapter is read aloud. Ask participants to close their eyes and get a mental picture of this scene. Ask them what they see and hear. Invite participants to turn to Genesis 11:1-9 and to follow along as you read aloud. Ask how these two stories are similar and different. Peter reviewed what the prophet Joel had said, that God declares, "I will pour out my Spirit upon all flesh." Ask the following questions:

- What are the implications of this story?
- What is the vision of Pentecost?
- How does our congregation embody that vision?
- Why should congregations of today return to the original vision of the church?
- What opportunities are emerging for our congregation in this area?

IV. Define key concepts

Copy and pass out the two charts on pages 136 and 137, "Expressions of Oppression (in the United States)" and "How the 'Isms' Play Out." Review the charts. Ask for questions or comments. Divide participants into small groups. Supply each group with newsprint and a marker. Ask each small group to think of one or two examples of each of the six ways the "isms" are played out (listed in bold on the chart) and write their examples on newsprint. Give the groups twenty minutes to work. Return to the large group and have the small groups report their examples. Discuss the meaning and consequences of racism, both active and passive. Explain the differences between assimilation and true appreciation of differences and between the images of the melting pot and the salad bowl. (The melting pot image suggests everything melts together while the salad bowl image portrays everything together but distinct.)

Break

V. Explore ethnic identity

This activity examines how we are a patchwork of cultures and ethnicities. Give participants an 8½-by-11-inch piece of paper, and ask them to fold it into four sections. In the four different sections of the paper have them describe the following aspects of their identity:

Section 1: Draw a picture or symbol representing where your ancestors are from.
Section 2: Draw a picture or describe how you identify yourself racially/ethnically.
Section 3: Describe an aspect of your racial/ethnic heritage that you are proud of.
Section 4: Describe in a word or phrase what you know about the heritage of your family or last name.

After participants have completed all four sections, ask each one to describe the "patches" on their "quilt" to the entire group. At the end of their descriptions, have the group tape their sheets together on the wall to form a group quilt. Discuss the process of this activity. Ask participants how easy or difficult it was to complete this activity. Ask what they learned about their sense of ethnic identity. Ask them how diverse they think the group is.

VI. Closing

Gather around the quilt. Review some of the expectations and fears expressed at the beginning of the class. See how those might be insightful for the next session. Sing, "Help Us Accept Each Other" (#560, *The United Methodist Hymnal*). Close with prayer.

Session 2: Understanding Community (Time needed: approximately 3 hours)

I. Gather and warm-up

Gather participants again and sing some lively songs. Invite participants to find someone they do not know very well and pair up with him or her. Ask each pair to interview each other using some or all of the following questions:

- Does our church have a mission? What is it? How would you describe it?
- What biblical passages or symbols are important for you and for your congregation and why?
- What holds your congregation together?
- What is something you have learned from or some way you have benefited from being a part of your congregation?

Have each pair share the results of the interview with the entire group.

II. Review goals and learnings from the previous session

III. Explore biblical understandings of community

Divide participants into small groups. Assign each group one of the following passages:

- Exodus 18
- Ruth 1
- John 4
- Mark 6:30-44
- Ephesians 4

Have each group answer the following questions about their passage and write their answers on newsprint. What does this passage say about community? About leadership? About crossing boundaries? (They may wish to use commentaries and other Bible helps.) Have each group report its findings to the large group.

Break

IV. Create a Bible epic

Acts 10:1-44. Introduce this story of the conversion of Cornelius to the large group. As a Jew, Peter believed his people to be God's chosen ones, so he followed the law that forbade him to associate with Gentiles. God showed him, however, that God has no partiality and loves all people equally. Depending on the size of your group, ask volunteers to take the following roles:

- Narrator
- Cornelius
- An angel
- Several slaves and soldiers
- Simon Peter

- Four-footed creature
- Birds
- Voice from heaven
- Cornelius's relatives and friends

Have the remainder of the participants be the audience. Give the players time to prepare and practice their role play. While they are doing that activity, have the audience prepare a stage. After the players have recreated the story, have participants debrief by talking about what this passage says about exclusivity and to their community.

V. Discuss
Write the following questions on newsprint, large enough for everyone to see. In the same small groups as before ask participants to decide on a spokesperson and discuss these questions:

- How much diversity is present in your congregation? What ethnic groups are represented?
- What is the view of your faith community toward racial and gender diversity?
- What cultural differences have been your biggest challenges?
- How diverse is the leadership of your congregation?
- How should we deal with prejudice within our congregation?
- What steps might be taken to broaden the congregation's understanding or to diversify leadership?

Allow small groups adequate time to reflect on these questions and have the spokespersons report highlights to the large group.

VI. Build a web of diversity
With the large group brainstorm a list of qualities and characteristics of community. Give each person an index card or piece of 8½-by-11-inch paper. Have them write one of the qualities on the piece of paper or card and tape it to themselves. Have the group stand in a circle and call out the name of one of the qualities. Throw a ball of multicolored yarn to the person wearing the respective card as each quality is called. Each person will hold a portion of the yarn, then continue passing the yarn until all qualities have been named. Repeat the procedure, this time have each person give a concrete example of that quality in action in his or her congregation. When the "web" is complete, take a group picture.

VII. Closing

Close with prayer.

Session 3: Sharing Leadership (Time needed: approximately 3 hours)

I. Gather and warm-up
Again, gather the group with some lively singing. Ask participants to pair up and ask each pair to make a list of qualities of a good church leader. When they have had sufficient time to do this task, ask participants to call out their qualities "popcorn style." Write these on newsprint as they call them out. Explain that you will be coming back to these later in the session.

II. Review goals and learnings so far

III. Explore gender stereotypes and attitudes toward gender
Returning to the concept of sexism from the first session, divide into small groups and ask the group to list gender

stereotypes on newsprint and discuss them: why they are harmful and how those are played out in the church. Give the group twenty minutes for this activity then have each group report on their discussion to the large group.

IV. Review women's leadership in the church

Ask the group: Women have an increasing presence in church leadership as both lay and clergy. How has that leadership affected the church? Ask if there are gender differences in leadership and what they are. Note the difference between differences and stereotypes.

Optional activities: You may have a knowledgeable person review some of the history of women's leadership and the ordination of women in your denomination, or you may tell the stories of several key women leaders in the history of your congregation.

V. Bible study

Divide into small groups. Instruct the groups to read Luke 18:1-8. Provide commentaries such as *The Women's Bible Commentary* by Carol Newsom and Sharon Ringe. Ask them to find out all they can about this parable. Ask them to list characteristics of the woman and how she exemplifies good leadership. Report back to the large group.

Then, ask the groups to turn to John 4:1-39. Again, ask them to find out all they can about the encounter of Jesus and the woman at the well. Have someone read verse 39 out loud. Ask what the significance of this woman's leadership is. Report to the large group.

Last, have the group turn to Galatians. 3:28. Ask the group to see what the commentaries say about this passage. Report to the large group. Ask for different translations of this verse to be read aloud.

Break

VI. Discuss leadership qualities

Return the large group's attention to their list of leadership qualities. Ask if there are others they would like to add. Ask how this list compares to the qualities of the women leaders in the church and in the Bible that were discussed previously. Assign each person one or more of the qualities. Have them think about how women exercise these qualities in the church. Ask them to name specific examples if they can. Instruct the participants to pair up with one or two other people and discuss their examples.

VII. Write a group covenant

Gather the large group in front of your quilt. Review learnings from each session. Tape all newsprint from previous sessions to the wall so that the group can see what has been discussed. Ask the group how they can resist the "isms" and embrace diversity. Ask how the faith community can share our leadership with people who are different. What might happen if we broadened our understanding of community and leadership? How might we become the church God intended us to be? Invite the group to write a covenant stating how they will promise to move toward this vision. Invite people to supply phrases for the covenant as you write them on newsprint. When the covenant is complete, close by singing "Help Us Accept Each Other" as participants come forward to sign the covenant.

Expressions of Oppression (in the United States)

variable	dominant group	subordinate group	ism
gender	men	women	sexism
race	white	people of color	racism
sexual orientation	heterosexual	lesbian, gay, bisexual	heterosexism
age	middle	young, old	ageism
ability	temporarily able-bodied	people with disabilities	ableism
class	middle-upper	poor, working	classism
religion	Christian	Jewish, Buddhist Moslem, etc.	anti-Semitic anti-. . .

Diversity Tool Kit © 1999 AAUW

How the "Isms" Play Out

Using Oppressive Language

• Using slurs such as "Indian giver," "girl" for woman, or "black" to mean bad as in "black sheep" or "blacklisted."

Maintaining Solidarity With Members of the Dominant Group

• Laughing at oppressive jokes.

• Backing up dominant group members when they act, talk, or tell jokes that are racist, sexist, etc. Backing up may include remaining silent or trying to minimize the behavior.

Excluding, Ignoring, Forgetting

• Not getting to know subordinate group members, learning their names, or greeting them.

• Not giving the same weight to their the ideas, opinions, and perspectives as you would to dominant group members.

• Expecting subordinate group members to know your name, your habits, and your needs.

Generalizing

• Viewing the mistakes of one subordinate group member as indicative of the whole group.

• Assuming that one subordinate group member or a few speak for the whole group.

• Noting that subordinate group members segregate thmselves, overlooking the fact that members of the dominant group have their own separate social groups.

Expecting to Be Taught

• Using subordinate group members to teach you about diversity and the "isms."

• Appointment only subordinate group members to committees on diversity.

Overprotecting

• Sheltering subordinate group members from failing or getting hurt.

• Making decisions for members of subordinate groups without asking their permission.

• Not interacting with subordinate group members for fear of saying the wrong thing.

Adapted with permission from materials by Deborah Kutenplon, Ellen Olmstead, and Deborah Piltch (Amherst: University of Massachusetts, S.C.E.R.A., the Student Center for Educational Research and Advocacy, 1987.

CHAPTER FIVE

The Web: How and Why It Could Work

Everybody knows when Spirit is up, and also when Spirit has disappeared. Wonderful things seem to happen when Spirit is present, and in its absence nothing much seems to take its place.

HARRISON OWEN, *THE SPIRIT OF LEADERSHIP*

The system is designed for the results it is getting. If you want different results, you have to change or improve the system.

EZRA EARL JONES, *QUEST FOR QUALITY*

For just as the body is one and has many members, and all the members of the body, though many, are one body, so it is with Christ. For in the one Spirit we were all baptized into one body—Jews or Greeks, slaves or free—and we were all made to drink of one Spirit.

1 CORINTHIANS 12:12-13

Now we take up the task of imagining how the web could work, hoping that we can stimulate the imaginations of our readers, whom we believe will be infinitely more innovative in implementing weblike leadership than we could be in our allotted space. How will this metaphor function for leadership in the church? What will it mean for our understanding of bishops and national church leadership? What will it mean for intermediary and regional leadership? How could the diaconate contribute to the implementation and success of the web, as we indicated in the first chapter?

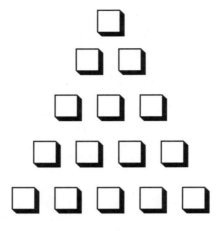

Figure 1

The typical organizational chart of most churches in America is some variation of figure 1. The Holy Spirit, if present at all, is in the background, and the CEO pastor at the top of the pyramid is in the foreground, front and

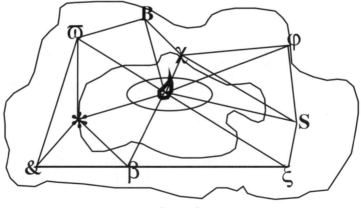

Figure 2

center. A web organization is more difficult to diagram and in many ways defies being reduced to an organizational chart but may look something like figure 2. The Holy Spirit is at the core, emanating outward.

A friend commented that this drawing resembles a Native American dreamcatcher. A dreamcatcher has a similar weblike center with the addition of traditional beads and feathers, and its story is inspiring. Hopi women made dreamcatchers, and they hung them over their sleeping children. As their children dreamed, the dream catcher would catch and hold their good dreams in its web. These would never be lost as long as they lived. An organizational chart is a long way from this beautiful art form, yet something is learned. Diverse people represent many good hopes and dreams. If we catch them and keep them, the church can receive blessings a hundredfold. If we let them go, as we have been doing, we lose much.

What If . . .

This section attempts to lay out some possibilities for what might be. None of these are exclusively "right" answers or principles to live by. Rather, they are beginnings that need further development, testing, and experience. Here, we are dreaming a bit about what might be, and we hope God's people may catch and hold some of these dreams. It is challenging and difficult to reconceptualize the way the church works and envision a system that will enable people to effectively and faithfully carry out the work of the church.

In examining community and diversity we came to realize that a community needs boundaries to *be* a community. It needs structure. We are not advocating trading one hierarchy for another or "throwing out the baby (community) with the bath water (hierarchy)." The rallying of the marginalized to leadership is not necessarily an achievement at the expense of others but an expedient response to a need for leadership with new ethical standards. One of the corporate women leaders that Sally Helgesen interviewed described the organizational structure of her company as "Jell-O pinned to the wall."[1] We want to emphasize the need for fluidity without abandoning the boundaries and the "gel" that forms us yet frees us to be community. We stress that in the church we have to be prepared to cross boundaries if necessary and to recognize that the boundaries may change.

Web leadership is becoming more operative the way many women in ministry are exercising this leadership, and many men also describe their own leadership in weblike terms. As this style of leadership becomes more operative there will be changes in church structure. We do not think there will be sudden and abrupt changes in structure, but more of an evolution. Some of what the future structure will look like depends on denominational needs and theological perspectives. We came up with ten key descriptive elements, which are as follows:

1) There will be less distinction between followers and leaders. Sometimes the usual leaders in a local congregation, or even in regional or national church leadership, will become followers, and the usual followers will find themselves leading and getting things done. Leadership will recreate and "make-over" the idea of following. Role reversal will mean that people who are used to taking charge will have to learn how to follow and support others. In actual function, the church could move away from the paradigm of a few key leaders doing everything because it subscribes to the myth that "nobody else will do it." Instead of filling slots or "volunteer" positions that the church structure dictates are necessary, we will make it possible for people to do what they are called to do, utilizing the gifts of the Body of Christ. Instead of the church structure dictating what is needed (the mission of the church), which is "the tail wagging the dog," the people will get to decide, and the needs (the mission), then, determine the structure. There will be a truer enactment of 1 Corinthians 12:12-13.

> You can easily enough see how this kind of thing works by looking no further than your own body. Your body has many parts—limbs, organs, cells—but no matter how many parts you can name, you're still one body. It's exactly the same with Christ. By means of his one Spirit, we all said goodbye to our partial and piecemeal lives. We each used to independently call our own shots, but then we entered into a large and integrated life in which *he* has the final say in everything. . . . Each of us is now a part of his resurrection body, refreshed and sustained at one fountain—his Spirit—where we all come to drink. The old labels we once used to identify ourselves—labels like Jew or Greek, slave or free—are no longer useful. *(The Message)*

Church staff and members will lead out of the gifts God has given to them, and staff and members will be interdependent upon one another. The roles of clergy and lay will be less defined. Staff persons may be paid because they are called to be a part of set apart ministry and to a church vocation for which they are trained and to which they devote themselves. *The Book of Discipline of the United Methodist Church* affirms that some persons are called from among the faithful to a set apart ministry. These people may be ordained, commissioned, consecrated, or certified by the church.

> The early church, through the laying on of hands, set apart persons with responsibility to preach, to teach, to administer the sacraments, to nurture, to heal, to gather the community in worship, and to send them forth in witness.

The church also set apart other persons to care for the physical needs of others, reflecting the concerns for the people of the world. In the New Testament (Acts 6), we see the apostles identifying and authorizing persons to a ministry of service. These functions, though set apart, we never separate from the ministry of the whole people of God.[2]

These persons will facilitate and inspire the members to be in ministry rather than doing all the ministry themselves. Members of the body will be "outfitted" to exercise relational power to lead the way. In a system like this, the Holy Spirit is at the center and at the margins, permeating the work of the community. The Spirit is the source of all the gifts and power needed so that no one needs to fight to get ahead. Nothing is gained by competing since the Spirit cannot be controlled. The management of the church will not be dominated by the values of the world as it has been; it will be dominated by the values emanating from the Holy Spirit's presence.

2) Social justice ministries will become the focus. Instead of being relegated to one department or committee, social justice ministries and mission will become the work of the whole body. There will be a connection that is obvious to all between the Sunday liturgy and the work of the church in the world. African American churches may serve as a model for this focus since social justice ministries are common in the African American church, with advocacy being almost second nature. Pastors of many African American churches are community activists. Vashti McKenzie writes that African American women tend to bring a care and concern for the African American community to whatever positions they hold in the church, looking for ways to incorporate a social justice perspective to their ministry.[3]

Clergy and laity will partner to form new social justice ministries. A huge Gothic church building stood nearly empty for twenty years as white people deserted the inner city. This church had a proud and impressive history and had been booming in its heyday (Sunday school classes had three and four hundred members). In recent years, however, only a few holdouts stayed loyal to the church because of family ties. Huge locks on every door kept the homeless out. There were few baptisms and many funerals. The church was doomed—that is until a bishop, in some stroke of genius (or insanity, according to some) sent the Reverend Juanita Wilson to pastor that church. She immediately spilled the worship services outside into the street, hosting Christian festivals with singing, praising, and rejoicing. Right in her own corridor she started a ministry with the homeless—feeding them, clothing them, and helping them find jobs. One or two laypeople caught the fever and joined in. Those they helped in turn helped others. Juanita connected with city groups to provide counseling and shelter for runaway teens and to host an AA meeting. Soon the church began to fill up again. Those outside were invited inside. Every Sunday was declared "Come As You Are" day. That meant that some came drunk, some came stoned, and many came dirty and unkempt. Juanita welcomed them all and gave them the good news in brilliant, living color. Some of the last diehards could not tolerate the changes and left, but some stayed—whether out of loyalty or curiosity, we do not know. The "them" and "us" attitude that had prevailed began to fade, as the "them" became the "us."

3) Worship will look very different. People will be involved and actually worshiping rather than watching the clergy perform. The cycle of "religious ritual" that George Barna described must be broken. According to the Barna Research Group more than one hundered million adults and thirty million children monthly come into contact with a Christian church.[4] Most of them, however, are involved in a religious ritual that provides little opportunity for connection to Christ. Hierarchical leaders of spectator ministries are a direct cause of this rote, meaningless ritualism that spiritually bankrupts the church. Eugene Peterson refers to these leaders as "branch manager[s] . . . in a religious warehouse outlet" who spend their lives "marketing God to religious consumers."[5]

Worship leadership will have to become more participatory, giving the ritual itself the chance to connect worshipers with the world. To some, participatory worship may appear more pentecostal or emotional. People will move more. They may clap. They may actually look like they are enjoying themselves! This will not suit some people. It's not to everyone's taste. It is easier, after all, to have some "private time" with God or to file in, sit down, and go through the motions without having to think. There will be moments of quiet and silence in worship, but there will always be a communal feeling to it. The people will experience a connection to God and to each other that will be evident. According to the *Spiritual Formation Bible,* relationships with other believers have extraordinary power in our lives because Jesus is present in them. People are important in conveying God's grace and presence, and one of the primary ways that we meet God is through community.[6] Worshipers cannot leave the sanctuary without being changed and challenged. The connection made in this ritual will affect how people live their lives all week.

4) Christian education will be for spiritual formation. There will be remarkable energy for Christian education, which web leadership will engender. Learning will not just be associated with Bible study or Sunday school but will be throughout the community and its work. Christian education will not be viewed as just for children or youth. All the life of the church will involve Christian education.

People will not just learn *about* God and the Bible; they will be given the freedom and opportunity to talk openly and explore their faith questions and struggles. People will grow in their faith and have a closer relationship with God, and community will be built. There will be many forms for this dialogue to take place. Specific times for group study, such as Sunday school, will not coincide with worship so that people will not have to choose. This "convenient" arrangement *always* sends the message that Sunday school is baby-sitting the kids while the adults go to church (implying that Sunday school is not church). The reality is that when Sunday school coincides with worship, most adults attend worship and not Sunday school, and they do not seek other opportunities for study and learning. In a renewed and reformatted understanding of Christian education, potential teachers who have been reluctant or underconfident will be called forth and will find their voice. There will be no more "dumbing down" in the church. It will be a center for theological and cultural discourse. We have already discussed the church as virtual seminary and acknowledging laypeople as theologians. The pedagogical styles that will engender this transformation are discussed in chapter 4.

5) Ministry will be done by small groups of people who covenant together. These mission groups will be able to define their own objectives and how to meet them rather than being appointed, defined, and judged by a superior in the "food chain." These covenant groups will not be committees bound by structure and hierarchically organized, but working groups for specific purposes. These groups will not be just teams that are project- or task-oriented and goal-driven, which tend to be short-lived. They will be webs, evolving slowly and based on relationships and connections. It may be difficult to distinguish who is the leader because there is no positional power attributed to a chairperson. People will take initiative and guide each other. In one church, a group of people with gifts of healing and caregiving have been organized. They were connected by a pastor who exercises web leadership. This group of people have become care partners and "connectors" in that congregation. They use phone-trees, E-mail, greeting cards, home visits, hugs, and prayers to stay connected to those who need care or just need to hear from a Christian friend. They connect people to each other face-to-face and, in so doing, to the living Christ.

People will come together and stay together to be in ministry. The church will hold together because of the strength of connection and diversity, not out of some sense of loyalty on the part of a few members. Loyalty implies fitting in and " 'fit in' was the mantra of the command-and-control structures of the Industrial Age."[7] Fitting together is a more accurate phrase for people in these groupings. The following "recipe for glue," provided by David Noer from a book on secular leadership, is suggested to facilitate this fitting together for ministry with "customer" being understood as people who come to the church seeking God's will for their lives:

> Fill the glue pot with the fresh, pure, clear water of undiluted human spirit.

Take special care not to contaminate with preconceived ideas, or to pollute with excess control.

Fill slowly; notice that the pot only fills from the bottom up. It's impossible to fill it from the top down!

Stir in equal parts of customer focus and pride in good work.

Bring to a boil and blend in a liberal portion of diversity, one part self-esteem, and one part tolerance.

Fold in accountability.

Simmer until smooth and thick, stirring with shared leadership and clear goals.

Season with a dash of humor and a pinch of adventure.

Let cool, then garnish with a topping of core values.

Serve by coating all boxes in the organizational chart, paying particular attention to the white spaces. With proper application, the boxes disappear.[8]

6) Reward systems will change or become unnecessary. People will not be rewarded because of how many new members they take in or how many meetings they can attend. People will be rewarded and receive blessing from the work itself and from fulfilling God's call. Of course, there will still be struggles, but part of the reward will be the support and love of the community. Pastors will not be rewarded by being sent to or by "getting" a bigger and better church with a higher salary. This "carrot dangling on a string" only serves to tempt pastors (they are human) to engage in untoward activities in order to get ahead. In some current systems, the best pastors, the "cream of the crop," get rewarded by being sent to churches that do not need them. We need proven pastors in the situations where there is the greatest challenge for ministry. Those competent and experienced pastors who can minister in the worst situations and redeem them are desperately needed in many places, but not in large, thriving, and wealthy churches.

We wrote in an earlier chapter about the evolution of the ascending scale or ladder in ministry. One of us knows a person who represents such a case of pure ambition in ministry. A pastor was sent to a declining urban congregation. Unlike Juanita, who redeemed a similar situation at an inner city church, this pastor, in his urgency to get ahead and get a better church, actually went to the town cemetery and copied down names of dead people then proceeded to take them in as members of the church. He reported an increase in membership to the hierarchy. He was, in fact, promoted in his denomination. Eugene Peterson says "we are awash in [vocational] idolatry . . . the idea of a religious career that we can take charge of and manage," the abandoning of vocation for a religious job.[9] Reward systems that either attract people to ministry who are self-promoting or cause people to become self-centered, competitive, and mostly interested in making themselves look good are destroying the church we love. Web leadership will have to overcome and transform this situation.

7) Churches will not stand alone, but will be more connected in districts, regions, and nations. Congregations will not have to reinvent wheel after wheel, but will join with other congregations and community organizations in carrying out ministry. District or regional organizations will facilitate the connections that will resemble a coalition. Churches will not try to outdo one another to look good, but will cooperate toward a jubilee vision when balances are restored, when balances of *power* and *relationship* are restored.

Skilled teachers, for example, may share their gifts with more than one congregation. A pool of lay teachers and speakers will be nurtured and will be a much needed resource to congregations. Members of more than one congregation will be able to come together to form a critical mass for Bible study or prayer or other learning opportunities without suspicion that one church is trying to steal members from another. We have much to learn from one another. Rather than having one or two district or regional heads, there will be a covenant group of leaders, including clergy and laypeople. District or regional leadership or leadership of a coalition of churches will not be a reward nor will these leaders have positional power.

8) Regional (conference) and national church leadership will not be top-heavy. More laypeople will be involved and feel ownership in decision making. In fact, the top-bottom mentality will disappear. More women will be seen in pivotal, national leadership roles, exercising web leadership and nurturing connections within the church.

Using a weblike leadership, conference leadership, church boards, and church agencies will operate differently. Boards will not be the authority and exert all the power of decision making; they will function as resources for the church. Today our churches are faced with problems that require fundamental changes in the way we think, plan, and act. We have noticed in our own work with national and conference boards that the board staff person or persons tend to do most of the talking. A nonhierarchical regional or conference board will value the opinions of each person, and all will feel free to communicate honestly without fear of the consequences. Instead of balkanization, trust would develop; the degree to which a board develops trust directly influences the success of that board. Dialogue will be questioning, thought provoking, and mutually empowering.

Conferences, synods, or conventions will be events that gather and connect people and emphasize worship and setting priorities for ministry for the coming years rather than events that focus on policy decisions and voting. A diagonal slice of the church would be represented. Instead of a preset agenda, organizers might have small group meetings prior to the larger session so everyone feels more involved and can help steer the direction of the conference.

For denominations that have bishops, the bishop's office will be more of a teaching role as opposed to an administrative one. In *By What Authority: A Conversation on Teaching Among United Methodists*, Thomas Langford points out "the lack of clear authority for determining the interrelationship of theology with worship and moral life."[10]

There is a real deficiency in the lack of teaching shepherds in the church; since our bishops are so confined to administrative duties and presiding over meetings as "executives in conference affairs,"[11] they are hard-pressed to be able to be guides in the spiritual formation of the Body of Christ. We heard someone say that to get elected bishop in the church today, you cannot have enemies. Not having enemies means making everybody happy and making them feel good at the expense of being prophetic. Administrative duties could be handled by officers of the general church, deacons, or others gifted in this ministry.

Bishops could derive and articulate an annual curriculum for the church based on theological discussions in conciliar bodies. A joint body of bishops, clergy, and laypeople, as an arm of the national or global church, could "run things," keep the machine going, and help the church stay connected. Bishops might serve for a term, possibly eight years, in the role of teaching bishop, then return to a parish or some other form of ministry before retirement. This would help to eliminate the "climb to the top" mentality. If the role of bishop is seen as more of a service and one form of the teaching ministry of the church, then there will be less of a hierarchical understanding of the episcopacy. Bishops, of course, will still have our respect and be authority figures, but more as mentors, spiritual directors, and servants and less as CEOs who deal in policy. Granted, the practice of electing a bishop for life is tradition, but it does not seem to us that the theological integrity of the episcopacy depends on being elected for life. Imagine the good that could be done in a parish or some other place by a bishop with his or her networks and connections.

9) The diaconate will have a pivotal role in web leadership in the church. A historic order of ministry in the church described in the New Testament, the diaconate has evolved over the years and has different expressions in different denominations and traditions. A deacon is a minister or servant, and the diaconate is an ecumenical concept. The World Federation of *Diakonia* unites deacons from most Christian traditions around the globe and supports their ministry.

In 1996 The United Methodist Church responded to a movement in the church to create a permanent order of deacons. Douglas Strong, professor of church history at Wesley Theological Seminary and chair of the Division of Deacons of the Baltimore-Washington Conference, says the church responded correctly "because of a disturbing lack of focus within the professional ministry, an intensifying dissatisfaction among religious leaders, [and] a deepening hunger for maturity at the center of our spirits." He believes the potential for the order is "one of the most exciting possibilities in years" if we do not politicize it too much.[12] If the church can resist the hierarchical urge to make the diaconate (deacons, deaconesses, and diaconal ministers) a second-class clergy and see it for its potential to jumpstart the church, then the mission and ministry of the church will be enhanced. Discussions about the future sacramental leadership of the deacon are ongoing as deacons increasingly find themselves in situations where authority to administer the sacraments is needed. We also believe that the reordering of ministry will contribute to the implementation and success of web leadership in the local church since a few of the primary roles of the deacon are equipper, resourcer, and teacher of the laity in their ministry. According to the World Council of Churches (WCC),

> Deacons represent to the Church its calling as servant in the world. By struggling in Christ's name with the myriad needs of societies and persons, deacons exemplify the interdependence of worship and service in the Church's life. They exercise responsibility in the worship of the congregation: for example by reading the scriptures, preaching, and leading the people in prayer. They help in the teaching of the congregation. They exercise a ministry of love within the community. They fulfill certain administrative tasks and may be elected to responsibilities for governance.[13]

Deacons will be a bridge between the church and the world. They will exercise connectional leadership according to Ormonde Plater in *Many Servants: An Introduction to Deacons.*

In a communal dimension, deacons bring their sign of ministry into the *koinonia* of the church. Through activity, word, and example, deacons encourage, enable, enlist, engage, entice, model, lead, animate, stimulate, inspire, inform, educate, permit, organize, equip, empower, and support Christian people in service in the world, and they point to the presence of Christ in the needy. They are signs of service who uncover and explain signs of service.[14]

Saint Lawrence, the patron saint of deacons, exemplified this connectional leadership in his relationship with the poor and marginalized. The story of Lawrence, a deacon in Rome during the third century, is told in *The Deacon: Ministry Through Words of Faith and Acts of Love*. Lawrence's bishop, who is also a good friend, is martyred in the persecution of Valerian. Lawrence himself is captured and arrested, and the tyrannical king demands that Lawrence turn over the riches of the church. He asks for a few days to "gather the riches." Lawrence then goes out into the streets and countryside and organizes the poor whom he knows well. He invites them to come to a large storehouse on a certain day and time for a meeting with the king. Although they are undoubtedly afraid, they trust Lawrence, so they show up on the agreed upon day. At the appointed time the king walks in to the storehouse expecting to find gold and silver. Lawrence gestures to the motley and diverse crowd of people before him and proclaims, "These are the riches of the church!" The king, however, did not appreciate the irony. Lawrence was martyred for his faith in 258 C.E.[15]

Saint Lawrence viewed the poor as the riches of the church, as assets rather than as "clients" in need of "servicing." He did not gather the poor as a show of his prowess, but rather he had the power to gather and organize the poor because of the strong relationships he

had built with them. The lesson for modern-day deacons, according to this book is that we must similarly
locate our power in relationships throughout the church
and the world.[16]

An ecumenical group of women in the diaconate, who
were gathered by the WCC, described their experience
of leadership in the church as using their experience of
marginalization to be a witness toward new ways of
shaping community. Some women who have been con-
ditioned to selfless service to the point that their sense of
self-worth was eliminated still affirmed a "no boundaries to compassion" guideline as a Christlike way to be
leaders in the church and eliminate oppression. The
group rearticulated the 1994 guidelines on the diakonia
by the Central Committee of the WCC as a way of
understanding it. The diakonia:

a) overcomes subordination of people;
b) is mutual because it expresses both our common and
   our diverse needs;
c) leads us to create a pathway that we can walk along
   together;
d) empowers and dignifies people to know and express
   themselves;
e) acknowledges each community's God-given right of
   self-determination;
f) challenges injustice in a holistic way through immediate and long-term actions;
g) preserves and shares the resources which sustain life;
h) nurtures and sustains communities in the place of
   marginalization and exclusion;
i) acknowledges the inevitable risks in restoring community through people who are learning to give, receive,
   ask, concede, compromise, lose, and so forth;
j) encourages us to be conscious of the contradictions
   between what we believe, ask, and do and challenges
   us to seek a deeper integrity;

k) expresses God's unlimited compassion, without abusing the dignity of the servant.[17]

10) Women's leadership will be valued and celebrated. In a new web structure for the church, gender will not be the defining factor in ministry. If a person brings the good news, preaches the gospel, and teaches with integrity, people will listen and gender will matter less. When more and more women rise in the church to speak or organize or dry some tears, there will be a loud chorus of amens. Women will not have to "hide" their gender or squelch their identities and personalities by trying to act like men. Instead their identities and personalities will bring something to the church that is badly needed— caring and connectional leadership.

Women ministers will model the best that women have to offer and will bring tremendous gifts to the church. Women will lead in the ways they are accustomed to, and those ways will be accepted and even appreciated. As a growing number of women occupy pulpits and church leadership posts there will be new role models that help to "democratize" our congregations and may even alter worshipers' traditional view of God as male.[18] Women leaders, women pastors, and women deacons will bring God to the people in a new, refreshing way. For now, large prestigious congregations still seem to prefer male senior pastors, but women and men who are not concerned with climbing the ladder to success and refuse to accept this kind of thinking will find ways to lead faithfully.

Seeds of Change

A global and inclusive community of the United Methodist Church was commissioned by the 1996 General Conference to manage, guide, and promote a transformation in the church. This group of people, called the Connectional Process Team (CPT), has completed a preliminary report in which they advocate some new organizational forms and refocus the church on spiritual formation. The CPT was charged with communicating and training toward an interactive organizational process. To do this, in order to help the church better carry out its mission, the team discerned eleven "transformational directions"—a somewhat awkward term for changes the church needs to make. These directions, some of which echo our key descriptors, include:

- Placing spiritual formation at the center of our work
- Invigorating the ministry of the church.
- Calling forth spiritual leaders.
- Creating a Covenant Council of spiritual and prophetic leaders.
- Empowering and nurturing the ministries of local congregations and faith communities.
- Recognizing the global nature of The United Methodist Church.
- Revitalizing the United Methodist connection.
- Strengthening ecumenical relationships.
- Structuring the general agencies to support congregations, faith communities, and annual conferences.
- Encouraging doctrinal and theological discourse.
- Being an inclusive church.[19]

The CPT recognized a shift from measuring the health of a congregation on the basis of the number of programs and committees to measuring its health on growth in faith and mission. The acknowledgment of the need to call forth spiritual leaders, which are described in weblike terms, and the creation of a Covenant Council as a centralized form of organization where lay and clergy work together were particularly striking. By eliminating all the segmented, bureaucratic committees of the local, district, and national church, the Covenant Council would guide the ministry of the church. The CPT is suggesting there be a Covenant Council in every conference, district, and local church. No function or task would be done in a church or stand separate from its Covenant Council. The style of the Covenant Council will be collegial and Spirit-driven.[20] The CPT also advocates a global United Methodist Conference that recognizes the need for understanding ourselves as a global community. Although we feel that the transformation document may not go far enough, we did find that the CPT tried to relay the concept that the church needs to understand how to put everything on the table so that everyone has a seat and the power does not rest with a few. We are not sure if the new structure they advocate will involve new leaders or simply rearrange already existing leadership. The team, led by Bishop Sharon Brown Christopher does reflect, however, the way women leaders are helping the church to think differently since the CPT recommendations demonstrate some very different ways of being the church.

General Conference 2000 did not endorse the CPT's recommendations for restructuring for more global and inclusive representation. However, delegates did support the transformational directions, which were mentioned earlier, on Christian formation, covenant leadership, connectional ministry, global and ecumenical dialogue, and theological dialogue. Though the status quo prevailed in regard to radically changing church structure, seeds were planted for more grassroots involvement, representation, and renewal. A focus group was established to research and evaluate emerging needs of the church.

In summary, we are suggesting that there is movement and momentum to change. However, we believe web leadership gives the "push" that powers the movement. The following chart illustrates the "directional flow":

FROM	TO
Hierarchical/Pyramid	Weblike structure
Linear	Circular
Analytical	Relational
Competition	Building community
Aristotelian logic	Cybernetics
Church growth	Church health
Authoritarian, "watch and listen" learning	Experiential, participatory, interactive learning
Fitting in	Fitting together

Words are one thing, but action is something else entirely. Our hope is we can walk the walk and not just talk the talk. Our hope is that the church we love will not just survive, but thrive and bloom. Our hope is that we have nurtured a tiny seed of change, and we leave you with this blessing:

Like the sea lapping against the shore,
We know that our future is coming to meet us.
Let us not be eroded by the floods of injustice,
but built up by time.
Let new life spring forth from the rock.
Let our springs not be silent, but
loudly and vibrantly green.
Amen.

Notes

1. The Web: What It Is and How It Feels

1. Jean Lipman-Blumen, *The Connective Edge: Leading in an Independent World* (San Francisco: Jossey-Bass Publishers, 1996), 10.

2. Sally Helgesen, *The Web of Inclusion: A New Architecture for Building Great Organizations* (New York: Doubleday, 1995), 20.

3. Mary Elizabeth Moore, "Poetry, Prophecy, and Power," *Religious Education* 93 (1998): 271.

4. Sallie McFague, *Models of God: Theology for an Ecological, Nuclear Age* (Philadelphia: Fortress Press, 1987), 24-28.

5. Mary Belenky et al., *Women's Way of Knowing: The Development of Self, Voice, and Mind* (New York: Basic Books, 1987), 178-79.

6. Stephen A. Rhodes, *Where the Nations Meet: The Church in a Multicultural World* (Downer's Grove, Ill.: InterVarsity Press, 1998), 199.

7. Sally Helgesen, *The Female Advantage: Women's Ways of Leadership* (New York: Doubleday, 1995).

8. Carlyle Murphy, "A Chorus of Amens As More Women Take Over Pulpits," *The Washington Post*, 25 July 1998, Metro section, p. B01.

9. Carol E. Becker, *Leading Women: How Church Women Can Avoid Leadership Traps and Negotiate the Gender Maze* (Nashville: Abingdon Press, 1996), 38-42.

10. Harriet Miller, "Women's Issues in Religious Education," in *Women's Issues in Religious Education*, Fern Giltner ed., (Birmingham, Ala.: Religious Education Press, 1985), 171-72.

11. Carol Gilligan, *In a Different Voice: Psychological Theory and Women's Development* (Cambridge: Harvard University Press, 1993).

12. Becker, *Leading Women*, 38-42.

13. Helgeson, *The Web of Inclusion*, 9-10.

14. Ibid., 126.

15. Alexandre Faivre, *The Emergence of the Laity in the Early Church* (New York: Paulist Press, 1990).

16. Margaret S. Wiborg and Elizabeth J. Collier, "United Methodist Clergywomen's Retention Study" (Anna Howard Shaw Center, Boston University School of Theology, October, 1997).

17. Constance Shehan and Marsha Wiggins, "University of Florida Study:

161

Female Ministers Face Pettiness, Patriarchy, and Pressures," *Sociological Focus* 32, no. 3 (August 1999): 247-263.

18. Leonard Sweet, *Soul Tsunami: Sink or Swim in the New Millennium Culture* (Grand Rapids: Zondervan, 1999), 19.

19. Faivre, *Emergence of the Laity*, 7.

20. Ibid., 15, 23.

21. Paulo Freire, *Pedagogy of the Oppressed* (New York: Seabury Press, 1968), 57-59.

22. Faivre, *Emergence of the Laity*, 147-49.

23. Mary Collins, "The Refusal of Women in Clerical Circles," in *Women in the Church*, vol. 1, ed. Madonna Kolbenschlag (Washington, D.C.: The Pastoral Press, 1987), 55.

24. Faivre, *Emergence of the Laity*, 46.

25. Maria Harris, *Fashion Me a People: Curriculum in the Church* (Louisville: Westminster/John Knox Press, 1989), 33.

26. Harold Recinos, *Who Comes in the Name of the Lord?* (Nashville: Abingdon Press, 1997).

27. Helgesen, *The Web of Inclusion*, 12, quoting Margaret Wheatley, *Leadership and the New Science: Learning About Organization from an Orderly Universe* (San Francisco: Berrett-Koehler, 1992), 17.

28. Ibid., 1-13.

29. Cheryl Sanders, *Ministry at the Margins: The Prophetic Mission of Women, Youth, and the Poor* (Downer's Grove: InterVarsity Press, 1997).

30. Rodney Hunter, *Dictionary of Pastoral Care and Counseling* (Nashville: Abingdon Press, 1990), 931.

31. Harrison Owen, *The Spirit of Leadership: Liberating the Leader in Each of Us* (San Francisco: Berrett-Koehler Publishers, 1999), 1.

32. Ibid., 2.

33. Ibid., 8.

34. B. Zikmund, B. A. Lummis, and P. Chang, *Clergy Women: An Uphill Calling* (Louisville: Westminster/John Knox Press, 1998), 51.

35. Ibid., 53.

36. Helgesen, *The Web of Inclusion*, 101-2.

37. Ibid., 115.

38. Eugene H. Peterson, *Subversive Spirituality* (Grand Rapids: William B. Eerdmans, 1997), 237-38.

39. Robin Maas, *Crucified Love: The Practice of Christian Perfection* (Nashville: Abingdon Press, 1989), 19.

40. Henri Nouwen, *In the Name of Jesus: Reflections on Christian Leadership* (New York: Crossroads, 1996), 37-39.

41. Helgesen, *The Web of Inclusion*, 38.

42. Ibid.

43. Nouwen, *In the Name of Jesus*, 15-17.

2. The Web and Spiritual Unity

1. M. Scott Peck, *The Different Drum: Community Making and Peace* (New York: Touchstone Books, 1988), 25-26.

2. Karen Jo Torjesen, *When Women Were Priests* (San Francisco: Harper and Row, 1993).

3. Catherine Wessinger, ed. *Religious Institutions and Women's Leadership* (Columbia: University of South Carolina Press, 1996).

4. Mary Collins, "Response to Orlando Espin" in *The Multicultural Church: A New Landscape in U.S. Theologies*, ed. William Cenkner (New York: Paulist Press, 1996), 74-75.

5. Vashti McKenzie, *Not Without a Struggle: Leadership Development for African American Women in Ministry* (Cleveland: United Church Press, 1996), 41.

6. Cain Hope Felder, *Troubling Biblical Waters* (New York: Orbis Books, 1989).

7. James Cone, *God of the Oppressed* (New York: Seabury Press, 1995), 39.

8. Dietrich Bonhoeffer, *Life Together* (New York: Harper and Row, 1954), 77.

9. Charles R. Foster, *Educating Congregations: The Future of Christian Education* (Nashville: Abingdon Press, 1994), 22.

10. Letty M. Russell, *Church in the Round: Feminist Interpretation of the Church* (Louisville: Westminster Press, 1993), 69.

11. Parker Palmer, *The Courage to Teach: Exploring the Inner Landscape of a Teacher's Life* (San Francisco: Jossey-Bass Publishers, 1998), 156.

12. Russell, *Church in the Round*, 11, 199.

13. Carlo Carretto, *The God Who Comes* (Maryknoll, N.Y.: Orbis Books, 1974), 183.

14. Audre Lorde, *Sister Outsider: Essays and Speeches* (New York: Crossing Press, 1984), 111.

15. Richard Louv, *The Web of Life: Weaving the Values that Sustain Us* (Berkeley: Conari Press, 1996), 3.

16. Ibid., 2.

17. Palmer, *Courage to Teach*, 96.

18. Russell, *Church in the Round*, 68.

19. McKenzie, *Not Without a Struggle*, 58.

20. Carol Lakey Hess, *Caretakers of Our Common House: Women's Development in Communities of Faith* (Nashville: Abingdon Press, 1997), 16.

21. Ibid., 216-17.

22. Renita Weems, *Just a Sister Away: A Womanist Vision of Relationships in the Bible* (San Diego: LuraMedia, 1998), 29.

23. Stephen A. Rhodes, *Where the Nations Meet: The Church in a Multicultural World* (Downer's Grove, Ill.: InterVarsity Press, 1998), 124.

24. Katherine Pfisterer Darr, *Far More Precious Than Jewels* (Louisville: Westminster/John Knox Press, 1991), 182.

25. Carol Newsom and Sharon Ringe, *The Women's Bible Commentary* (London: SPCK, 1992), 133.

26. Hess, *Caretakers*, 212.

27. Stephen V. Doughty, *Discovering Community* (Nashville: Upper Room Books, 1999), 109.

28. Osvaldo Vena, unpublished lecture, Association of Professors and Researchers in Religious Education Conference, 1999.

29. Parker Palmer, *The Active Life: Wisdom for Work, Creativity, and Caring* (San Francisco: HarperSanFrancisco, 1990), 123.

30. Ibid., 130.

31. Ibid., 132.

32. Ibid., 132, 136.

33. Gerrit Scott Dawson, *Called by a New Name* (Nashville: Upper Room Books, 1997), 14.

34. Peck, *Different Drum*, 61-62.

35. Flora Slosson Wuellner, *Feed My Shepherds* (Nashville: Upper Room Books, 1998), 157.

36. Julia Esquivel, *Threatened with Resurrection*, 2nd edition, trans. Anne Woehrle (Elgin, Ill.: Brethren Press, 1994), 63.

37. Wuellner, *Feed My Shepherds*, 154.

38. Charles V. Bryant, *Rediscovering Our Spiritual Gifts* (Nashville: Upper Room Books, 1991), 15.

39. Robin Maas, *Crucified Love: The Practice of Christian Perfection* (Nashville: Abingdon Press, 1989), 19-20.

40. Sally Helgesen, *The Web of Inclusion: A New Architecture for Building Great Organizations* (New York: Doubleday, 1995), 24-32.

41. Leonard Sweet, *Soul Tsunami: Sink or Swim in the New Millennium Culture* (Grand Rapids: Zondervan, 1999), 243.

42. Harrison Owen, *The Spirit of Leadership: Liberating the Leader in Each of Us* (San Francisco: Berrett-Koehler Publishers, 1999), 10-13.

43. Russell, *Church in the Round*, 20.

3. The Web and Diversity

1. Alan Segal, *Paul the Convert: The Apostolate and the Apostasy of Saul the Pharisee* (New Haven: Yale University Press, 1990), 174.

2. Stephen A. Rhodes, *Where the Nations Meet: The Church in a Multicultural World* (Downer's Grove, Ill.: InterVarsity Press, 1998), 11.

3. Ibid., 75.

4. Charles R. Foster and Theodore Brelsford, *We Are the Church Together: Cultural Diversity in Congregational Life* (Valley Forge, Pa.: Trinity Press International, 1996), 1.

5. American Association of University Women, *Diversity Tool Kit* (Washington, D.C.: AAUW, 1999), 4.

6. Charles R. Foster, *Educating Congregations: The Future of Christian Education* (Nashville: Abingdon Press, 1994), 21.

7. Miroslav Volf, *Exclusion and Embrace: A Theological Exploration of Identity, Otherness, and Reconciliation* (Nashville: Abingdon Press, 1996), 36.

8. Fumitaka Matsuoka, *The Color of Faith: Building Community in a Multiracial Society* (Cleveland: United Church Press, 1998), 7.

9. Letty M. Russell, *Church in the Round: Feminist Interpretation of the Church* (Louisville: Westminster Press, 1993), 158.

10. Harold Recinos, *Who Comes in the Name of the Lord?* (Nashville: Abingdon Press, 1997), 20.

11. Volf, *Exclusion and Embrace*, 17.

12. Parker Palmer, *The Courage to Teach: Exploring the Inner Landscape of a Teacher's Life* (San Francisco: Jossey-Bass Publishers, 1998), 37.

13. Ibid., 38.

14. Mary Catherine Bateson, *Peripheral Vision: Learning Along the Way* (New York: HarperCollins, 1994), 23.

15. Volf, *Exclusion and Embrace*, 36.

16. Ibid., 75-77.

17. Foster and Brelsford, *We Are the Church*, 18.

18. AAUW, *Diversity Tool Kit*, 1.

19. Foster and Brelsford, 3.

20. Russell, *Church in the Round*, 160.

21. Ibid., 195.

22. Volf, *Exclusion and Embrace*, 74-75.

23. Matsuoka, *Color of Faith*, 29.

24. Russell, *Church in the Round,* 73.
25. Matsuoka, *Color of Faith,* 125, quoting Coretta Scott King, *The Words of Martin Luther King Jr.* (New York: Newsmaker Press, 1983), 65.
26. Greer Anne Wenh-In Ng, "Toward a Theology of Solidarity," in *Groundswell: Ecumenical Decade—Churches in Solidarity with Women* (Toronto: Canadian Council of Churches, 1996), 1-2.
27. bell hooks, "Choosing the Margin As a Space of Radical Openness," in *Yearning: Race, Gender, and Cultural Politics* (Toronto: Between the Lines Press, 1990), 145-53.
28. Maurianne Adams, Lee Anne Bell, and Pat Griffin, eds., *Teaching for Diversity and Social Justice: A Sourcebook* (New York: Routledge Press, 1997), 91.
29. Paulo Freire, *Pedagogy of the Oppressed* (New York: Seabury Press, 1968), 33.
30. Rhodes, *Where the Nations Meet,* 25-26.
31. Adams, Bell, and Griffin, *Teaching for Diversity,* 4-9.
32. Deborah Tannen, *You Just Don't Understand: Women and Men in Conversation* (New York: Ballantine Books, 1990), 17.
33. Carol E. Becker, *Leading Women: How Church Women Can Avoid Leadership Traps and Negotiate the Gender Maze* (Nashville: Abingdon Press, 1996), 54-56, 129.
34. Sally B. Purvis, *The Stained Glass Ceiling: Churches and Their Women Pastors* (Louisville: Westminster/John Knox Press, 1995), 31.
35. Deborah L. Sheppard et al., eds., *The Sexuality of Organization* (London: Sage Publications, 1989), 145.
36. Matsuoka, *Color of Faith,* 5.
37. Rebecca Chopp, *The Power to Speak: Feminism, Language, God* (New York: Crossroad, 1989), 2.
38. Margaret S. Wiborg and Elizabeth J. Collier, "United Methodist Clergywomen's Retention Study" (Anna Howard Shaw Center, Boston University School of Theology, October, 1997), 78-79, 17.
39. Ibid., 19.
40. C-4 Study, "The Collier Study" (a report of the Division of Ordained Ministry, General Board of Higher Education, 1989).
41. Statistical analysis of the data may be found in the United Methodist Clergywomen Retention Study report published by the Division of Ordained Ministry, General Board of Higher Education and Ministry, The United Methodist Church.
42. Frederick W. Schmidt, *A Still Small Voice: Women, Ordination and the Church* (New York: Syracuse University Press, 1996), 2.
43. Ibid., 17.
44. Delores Carpenter, lecture, The Feminine in Religious Traditions Series, Howard University School of Divinity, 1997.
45. Bernice Johnson Reagon, "Sing O Barren One," *Sacred Ground,* Songtalk Publishing Company, 1995.
46. Ibid.
47. Tannen, *You Just Don't Understand,* 42.
48. Edward Robinson, Jonathan Hickman, et al., "Where Diversity Really Works," *Fortune* (19 July 1999): 52, 60, 62, 68.
49. David A. Thomas and Robin Ely, "Making Differences Matter: A New Paradigm," *Harvard Business Review* (September/October 1996): 79-80, 83, 85.
50. Becker, *Leading Women,* 38-42.
51. Tannen, *You Just Don't Understand,* 45, 51.

52. Foster, *Educating Congregations*, 16.
53. Foster and Brelsford, *We Are the Church*, 120-26.
54. Foster, *Educating Congregations*, 126.
55. Eric H. F. Law, *The Wolf Shall Dwell with the Lamb: A Spirituality for Leadership in a Multicultural Community* (St. Louis: Chalice Press, 1993), 3.
56. Matsuoka, *Color of Faith*, 5.
57. Foster, *Educating Congregations*, 122.
58. David W. Augsburger, *Pastoral Counseling Across Cultures* (Philadelphia: Westminster Press, 1986).
59. Foster, *Educating Congregations*, 119-20.
60. Rhodes, *Where the Nations Meet*, 17.
61. Carpenter, lecture.

4. The Web and Pedagogy

1. Maurianne Adams, Lee Anne Bell, and Pat Griffin, eds., *Teaching for Diversity and Social Justice: A Sourcebook* (New York: Routledge Press, 1997), 4.
2. Jorge Acevedo, "Beyond the Lectionary," *Circuit Rider* (July-August 1999): 13.
3. Ibid.
4. Evans E. Crawford and Thomas H. Troeger, *The Hum: Call and Response in African American Preaching* (Nashville: Abingdon Press, 1995), 55-57.
5. Leonard Sweet, *Soul Tsunami: Sink or Swim in the New Millennium Culture* (Grand Rapids: Zondervan, 1999), 212.
6. James Smart, *The Teaching Ministry of the Church* (Philadelphia: Westminster Press, 1954).
7. Ronnie Prevost, "The Prophetic Voice of the Religious Educator," *Religious Education* 93 (summer 1998): 304.
8. Kathleen Weiler, *Women Teaching for Change: Gender, Class, and Power* (New York: Bergin and Garvey Publishers, 1988), 5.
9. Parker Palmer, *To Know As We Are Known: A Spirituality of Education* (San Francisco: Harper and Row, 1983), 2.
10. Ibid., 5.
11. Ibid., 33.
12. Harold Recinos, *Who Comes in the Name of the Lord?* (Nashville: Abingdon Press, 1997), 39.
13. Palmer, *To Know*, 39.
14. Maria Harris, *Fashion Me a People: Curriculum in the Church* (Louisville: Westminster/John Knox Press, 1989), 19.
15. Parker Palmer, *The Courage to Teach: Exploring the Inner Landscape of a Teacher's Life* (San Francisco: Jossey-Bass Publishers, 1998), 36.
16. Palmer, *To Know*, 38-39.
17. Mary Belenky et al. *Women's Way of Knowing: The Development of Self, Voice, and Mind* (New York: Basic Books, 1987), 35, 44, 101, 116.
18. Palmer, *To Know*, 8.
19. Ibid., 9.
20. Palmer, *The Courage to Teach*, 95.
21. Mary Elizabeth Moore, *Teaching from the Heart: Theology and Educational Method* (Minneapolis: Fortress Press, 1991), 2, 213.
22. Adams, Bell, And Griffin, *Teaching for Diversity*, 37.
23. Nelle Morton, *The Journey Is Home* (Boston: Beacon Press, 1985), 55-56.

24. Sally Helgesen, *The Web of Inclusion: A New Architecture for Building Great Organizations* (New York: Doubleday, 1995), 6.

25. Ibid, 18.

26. Harris, *Fashion Me a People*, 69.

27. Belenky, *Women's Way of Knowing*, 112-13.

28. Weiler, *Women Teaching for Change*, 58.

29. Palmer, *To Know*, 66.

30. Adams, Bell, And Griffin, *Teaching for Diversity*, 34, quoting Gloria Ladson-Billings "Toward a Theory of Culturally Relevant Pedagogy," *American Educational Research Journal* 32, 3 (1995): 482.

31. David Kolb, *Experiential Learning: Experience As the Source of Learning and Development* (Englewood Cliffs, N.J.: Prentice Hall, 1984).

32. Thomas H. Groome, *Christian Religious Education: Sharing Our Story and Vision* (San Francisco: Harper and Row, 1980), 184.

33. Ibid., 184-97.

34. Palmer, *To Know*, 107.

35. Palmer, *The Courage to Teach*, 11.

36. Moore, *Teaching from the Heart*, 2, 131.

37. Stephen V. Doughty, *Discovering Community* (Nashville: Upper Room Books, 1999), 72.

38. Palmer, *The Courage to Teach*, 58.

39. Mary Catherine Bateson, *Peripheral Vision: Learning Along the Way* (New York: HarperCollins, 1994), 211-12.

40. Leonard Sweet, *Soul Tsunami: Sink or Swim in the New Millennium Culture* (Grand Rapids: Zondervan, 1999), 206.

41. Ibid., 206.

42. Bateson, *Peripheral Vision*, 30.

43. Janice E. Hale-Benson, *Black Children: Their Roots, Culture, and Learning Styles* (Baltimore: Johns Hopkins University Press, 1986), 31.

44. Barbara Omolade, "A Black Feminist Pedagogy," *Women's Studies Quarterly* 15 (1987): 3-4.

5. The Web: How and Why It Could Work

1. Sally Helgesen, *The Web of Inclusion: A New Architecture for Building Great Organizations* (New York: Doubleday, 1995), 25.

2. *The Book of Discipline of the United Methodist Church 1996* (Nashville: The United Methodist Publishing House, 1996), pars. 302, 170.

3. Vashti McKenzie, *Not Without a Struggle: Leadership Development for African American Women in Ministry* (Cleveland: United Church Press, 1996), 72.

4. Leonard Sweet, *Soul Tsunami: Sink or Swim in the New Millennium Culture* (Grand Rapids: Zondervan, 1999), 50.

5. Eugene H. Peterson, *Under the Unpredictable Plant: An Exploration in Vocational Holiness* (Grand Rapids: Eerdmans, 1992), 38.

6. *The Spiritual Formation Bible* (Grand Rapids: Zondervan Press,1999), 1498.

7. Sweet, *Soul Tsunami*, 300.

8. David M. Noer, "A Recipe for Glue," in *The Leader of the Future*, Hesselbein, Goldsmith, and Beckhard, eds. (San Francisco: Jossey-Bass Publishers, 1996), 144-45.

9. Peterson, *Under the Unpredictable Plant*, 4.

10. Thomas A. Langford, "Teaching in the Methodist Tradition: A Wesleyan

Perspective," in *By What Authority: A Conversation on Teaching Among United Methodists*, Price and Foster, eds. (Nashville: Abingdon Press, 1991), 58.

11. Ibid., 60.

12. Douglas Strong, "So What? Living into Vocational Holiness," address from the convening of the orders of Deacons and Elders (Baltimore-Washington Conference, United Methodist Church, 1998).

13. *Baptism, Eucharist, and Ministry*, Faith and Order paper, no. 11 (Geneva: World Council of Churches, 1982).

14. Ormonde Plater, *Many Servants: An Introduction to Deacons* (Boston: Cowley Publications, 1991), 122.

15. Ben L. Hartley and Paul Van Buren, *The Deacon: Ministry Through Words of Faith and Acts of Love* (Nashville: General Board of Higher Education and Ministry, 1999), 31-32.

16. Ibid.

17. Myra Blyth and Wendy Robins, *No Boundaries to Compassion? An Exploration of Women, Gender, and Diakonia* (Geneva: World Council of Churches, 1988), 75.

18. Carlyle Murphy, "A Chorus of Amens As More Women Take Over Pulpits," *The Washington Post*, 25 July 1998, Metro section, p. B01.

19. "Transitional Directions for the United Methodist Church for the Twenty-first Century," report presented by the Correctional Process Team; available at www.umc.org/cpt/report/default.htm; INTERNET.

20. Ibid.

Bibliography

Acevedo, Jorge. "Beyond the Lectionary." *Circuit Rider* (July-August 1999): 13.

Adams, Maurianne, Lee Anne Bell, and Pat Griffin, eds. *Teaching for Diversity and Social Justice: A Sourcebook*. New York: Routledge Press, 1997.

Augsburger, David W. *Pastoral Counseling Across Cultures*. Philadelphia: Westminster Press, 1986.

Bateson, Mary Catherine. *Peripheral Vision: Learning Along the Way*. New York: HarperCollins, 1994.

Becker, Carol E. *Leading Women: How Church Women Can Avoid Leadership Traps and Negotiate the Gender Maze*. Nashville: Abingdon Press, 1996.

Belenky, Mary, et al. *Women's Ways of Knowing: The Development of Self, Voice, and Mind*. New York: Basic Books, 1986.

Blyth, Myra, and Wendy Robins. *No Boundaries to Compassion? An Exploration of Women, Gender, and Diakonia*. Geneva: World Council of Churches Publications, 1988.

Bondi, Richard. *Leading God's People: Ethics for the Practice of Ministry*. Nashville: Abindgon Press, 1989.

Bonhoeffer, Dietrich. *Life Together*. New York: Harper and Row, 1954.

Bryant, Charles V. *Rediscovering Our Spiritual Gifts*. Nashville: Upper Room Books, 1991.

Buber, Martin. *I and Thou*. Edinburgh: T and T Clark, 1970.

Carpenter, Delores. *Profile of Black Female Master of Divinity Graduates, 1972–1989*. Paper presented for the Feminine in Religious Traditions lecture series at Howard University School of Divinity, Washington, D.C., 1997.

Carretto, Carlo. *The God Who Comes*. Maryknoll, N.Y.: Orbis Books, 1974.

Cenkner, William, ed. *The Multicultural Church: A New Landscape in U.S. Theologies*. New York: Paulist Press, 1996.

Chopp, Rebecca. *The Power to Speak: Feminism, Language, God*. New York: Crossroad, 1989.

Collins, Mary. "The Refusal of Women in Clerical Circles." In *Women in the Church*. Vol. 1, ed. Madonna Kolbenschlag. Washington, D.C.: The Pastoral Press, 1987.

Cone, James. *God of the Oppressed*. New York: Seabury Press, 1975.

Crawford, Evans E, and Thomas H. Troeger. *The Hum: Call and Response in African American Preaching*. Nashville: Abingdon Press, 1995.

Culley, Margo. *Gendered Subjects: The Dynamics of Feminist Teaching*. Boston: Routledge and Kegan, 1985.

Darr, Katherine Pfisterer. *Far More Precious Than Jewels*. Louisville: Westminster/John Knox Press, 1991.

Dawson, Gerrit Scott. *Called by a New Name*. Nashville: Upper Room Books, 1997.

Doughty, Stephen V. *Discovering Community*. Nashville: Upper Room Books, 1999.

Edge, Findley. *The Greening of the Church*. Waco, Tex.: Word Books, 1971.

Esquivel, Julia. *Threatened with Resurrection*. Elgin, Ill.: The Brethren Press, 1982.

Faivre, Alexandre. *The Emergence of the Laity in the Early Church*. New York: Paulist Press, 1990.

Felder, Cain Hope. Lecture delivered at Kelly Miller Smith Institute, Vanderbilt University, Nashville, Tenn., October 1992.

———. *Stony the Road We Trod: African American Biblical Interpretation*. Minneapolis: Fortress Press, 1991.

Foster, Charles R. *Educating Congregations: The Future of Christian Education*. Nashville: Abingdon Press, 1994.

———, and Theodore Brelsford. *We Are the Church Together: Cultural Diversity in Congregational Life*. Valley Forge, Pa.: Trinity Press International, 1996.

Freire, Paulo. *Pedagogy of the Oppressed*. New York: Seabury Press, 1968.

Gilligan, Carol. *In a Different Voice: Psychological Theory and Women's Development*. Cambridge: Harvard University Press, 1993.

Giltner, Fern. *Women's Issues in Religious Education*. Birmingham, Ala.: Religious Education Press, 1985.

Groome, Thomas H. *Christian Religious Education: Sharing Our Story and Vision*. San Francisco: Harper and Row, 1980.

Hale-Benson, Janice E. *Black Children: Their Roots, Culture, and Learning Styles*. Baltimore: Johns Hopkins University Press, 1986.

Harris, Maria. *Fashion Me a People: Curriculum in the Church*. Louisville: Westminster/John Knox Press, 1989.

———. *Women and Teaching: Themes for a Spirituality of Pedagogy*. New York: Paulist Press, 1988.

Hartley, Ben L., and Paul Van Buren. *The Deacon: Ministry Through*

Words of Faith and Acts of Love. Nashville: General Board of Higher Education and Ministry, 1999.

Helgesen, Sally. *The Female Advantage: Women's Ways of Leadership*. New York: Doubleday, 1995.

———. *The Web of Inclusion: A New Architecture for Building Great Organizations*. New York: Doubleday, 1995.

Hess, Carol Lakey. *Caretakers of Our Common House: Women's Development in Communities of Faith*. Nashville: Abingdon Press, 1997.

hooks, bell. "Choosing the Margin As a Space of Radical Openness." In *Yearning: Race, Gender, and Cultural Politics*. Toronto: Between the Lines Press, 1990.

Hunter, Rodney. *Dictionary of Pastoral Care and Counseling*. Nashville: Abingdon Press, 1990.

Johnson, David, and Jeff VanVonderen. *The Subtle Power of Spiritual Abuse*. Minneapolis: Bethany House Publishers, 1970.

Jones, Ezra Earl. *Quest for Quality*. Nashville: Discipleship Resources, 1993.

Kolb, David. *Experiential Learning: Experience as the Source of Learning and Development*. Englewood Cliffs, N.J.: Prentice Hall, 1984.

Kraemer, Hendrik. *A Theology of the Laity*. Philadelphia: Westminster Press, 1958.

Langford, Thomas A. "Teaching in the Methodist Tradition: A Wesleyan Perspective." In *By What Authority: A Conversation on Teaching Among United Methodists*, edited by Elizabeth B. Price and Charles R. Foster. Nashville: Abingdon Press, 1991.

Law, Eric H. F. *The Wolf Shall Dwell with the Lamb: A Spirituality for Leadership in a Multicultural Community*. St. Louis: Chalice Press, 1993.

Lipman-Blumen, Jean. *The Connective Edge: Leading in an Independent World*. San Francisco: Jossey-Bass Publishers, 1996.

Lorde, Audre. *Sister Outsider: Essays and Speeches*. New York: Crossing Press, 1984.

Louv, Richard. *The Web of Life: Weaving the Values that Sustain Us*. Berkeley: Conari Press, 1996.

Maas, Robin. *Church Bible Study Handbook*. Nashville: Abingdon Press, 1982.

———. *Crucified Love: The Practice of Christian Perfection*. Nashville: Abingdon Press, 1989.

McClelland, David. *Power: The Inner Experience*. New York: Irvington Publishers, 1975.

McFague, Sallie. *Models of God: Theology for an Ecological, Nuclear Age*. Philadelphia: Fortress Press, 1987.

McKenzie, Vashti. *Not Without a Struggle: Leadership Development for African American Women In Ministry*. Cleveland: United Church Press, 1996.

Matsuoka, Fumitaka. *The Color of Faith: Building Community in a Multiracial Society.* Cleveland: United Church Press, 1998.

Moore, Mary Elizabeth. "Poetry, Prophecy, and Power." *Religious Education* 93 (1998): 271.

———. *Teaching from the Heart: Theology and Educational Method.* Minneapolis: Fortress Press, 1991.

Morton, Nelle. *The Journey Is Home.* Boston: Beacon Press, 1985.

Murphy, Caryle. "A Chorus of Amens As More Women Take Over Pulpits." *The Washington Post,* 25 July 1998.

Niebuhr, Richard. *The Purpose of the Church and Its Ministry.* New York: Harper and Row, 1956.

Newsom, Carol, and Sharon Ringe. *The Women's Bible Commentary.* London: SPCK, 1992.

Ng, Greer Anne Wenh-In. "Toward a Theology of Solidarity." In *Groundswell: Ecumenical Decade—Churches in Solidarity with Women.* Toronto: Canadian Council of Churches, 1996.

Noer, David M. "A Recipe for Glue." In *The Leader of the Future,* Hesselbein, edited by Goldsmith, and Beckhard. San Francisco: Jossey-Bass Publishers, 1996.

Nouwen, Henri. *In the Name of Jesus: Reflections on Christian Leadership.* New York: Crossroad, 1996.

Omolade, Barbara. "A Black Feminist Pedagogy." *Women's Studies Quarterly.* (1987): 3, 4, 15.

Owen, Harrison. *The Spirit of Leadership: Liberating the Leader in Each of Us.* San Francisco: Berrett-Koehler Publishers, 1999.

Palmer, Parker. *The Active Life: Wisdom for Work, Creativity, and Caring.* San Francisco: Harper and Row, 1990.

———. *The Courage to Teach: Exploring the Inner Landscape of a Teacher's Life.* San Francisco: Jossey-Bass, 1998.

———. *To Know As We Are Known: A Spirituality of Education.* San Francisco: Harper and Row, 1983.

Peck, M. Scott. *The Different Drum: Community Making and Peace.* New York: Touchstone Books, 1988.

Peterson, Eugene H. *The Message.* Colorado Springs: NavPress, 1995.

———. *Subversive Spirituality.* Grand Rapids: William B. Eerdmans Publications, 1997.

———. *Under the Unpredictable Plant: An Exploration in Vocation Holiness.* Grand Rapids: Eerdmans, 1992.

Plater, Ormonde. *Many Servants: An Introduction to Deacons.* Boston: Cowley Publications, 1991.

Prevost, Ronnie. "The Prophetic Voice of the Religious Educator." *Religious Education.* 93 (summer 1998): 3.

Purvis, Sally B. *The Stained Glass Ceiling: Churches and Their Women Pastors.* Louisville: Westminster/John Knox Press, 1995.

Recinos, Harold. *Who Comes in the Name of the Lord?* Nashville: Abingdon Press, 1997.

Richards, Lawrence O., and Clyde Hoeldtke. *A Theology of Church Leadership*. Grand Rapids: Zondervan, 1980.

Rhodes, Stephen A. *Where the Nations Meet: The Church in a Multicultural World*. Downer's Grove, Ill.: InterVarsity Press, 1998.

Russell, Letty M. *Church in the Round: Feminist Interpretation of the Church*. Louisville: Westminster Press, 1993.

Sanders, Cheryl. *Saints in Exile: The Holiness-Pentecostal Experience in African American Religion and Culture*. New York: Oxford University Press, 1996.

Schmidt, Frederick W. *A Still, Small Voice: Women, Ordination, and the Church*. New York: Syracuse University Press, 1996.

Segal, Alan. *Paul the Convert: The Apostolate and the Apostasy of Saul the Pharisee*. New Haven: Yale University Press, 1990.

Sheppard, Deborah L., et al., eds. *The Sexuality of Organization*. London: Sage Publications, 1989.

Smart, James. *The Teaching Ministry of the Church*. Philadelphia: Westminster Press, 1954.

Socrates. *Apologia*. Boston: Ginn and Company, 1895.

The Spiritual Formation Bible. Grand Rapids: Zondervan, 1999.

Strong, Douglas. "So What? Living into Vocational Holiness." Address for the convening of the orders of Deacons and Elders. Baltimore-Washington Conference, United Methodist Church, 1998.

Sweet, Leonard. *Soul Tsunami: Sink or Swim in the New Millennium Culture*. Grand Rapids: Zondervan, 1999.

Tannen, Deborah. *You Just Don't Understand: Women and Men in Conversation*. New York: Ballantine Books, 1990.

Thomas, David A., and Ely, Robin. "Making Differences Matter: A New Paradigm." *Harvard Business Review* (September/October 1996): 79.

Tiffany, Frederick C., and Sharon Ringe. *Biblical Interpretation: A Roadmap*. Nashville: Abingdon Press, 1996.

Torjesen, Karen Jo. *When Women Were Priests*. San Francisco: Harper and Row, 1993.

The United Methodist Hymnal. Nashville: The United Methodist Publishing House, 1989.

Volf, Miroslav. *Exclusion and Embrace: A Theological Exploration of Identity, Otherness, and Reconciliation*. Nashville: Abingdon Press, 1996.

Weiler, Kathleen. *Women Teaching for Change: Gender, Class, and Power*. New York: Bergin and Garvey Publishers, 1988.

Weems, Renita. *Just a Sister Away: A Womanist Vision of Relationships in the Bible*. San Diego: LuraMedia, 1988.

Wessinger, Catherine, ed. *Religious Institutions and Women's Leadership*. Columbia: University of South Carolina Press, 1996.

Wiborg, Margaret S. and Collier, Elizabeth J. "United Methodist Clergywomen's Retention Study." Anna Howard Shaw Center,

Boston University School of Theology, October 1997. (Division of Ordained Ministry, General Board of Higher Education and Ministry, The United Methodist Church.)

Williams, Delores S. *Sisters in the Wilderness: The Challenge of Womanist God-talk*. Maryknoll, N.Y.: Orbis Books, 1993.

Wilson, Marlene. *How to Mobilize Church Volunteers*. Minneapolis: Augsburg Fortress, 1983.

Wuellner, Flora Slosson. *Feed My Shepherds*. Nashville: Upper Room Books, 1998.

Zikmund, B., A. Lummis, and P. Chang. *Clergy Women: An Uphill Calling*. Louisville: Westminster/John Knox Press, 1998.